Low Cholesterol, Lower Calorie
French
Cooking

low cholesterol, lower calorie
French Cooking

Stanley Leinwoll

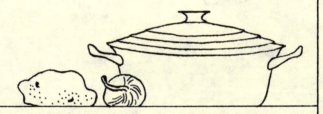

Charles Scribner's Sons   **New York**

For Miriam, Laura, and Joan

Copyright © 1974 Stanley Leinwoll

Library of Congress Cataloging in Publication Data

Leinwoll, Stanley.
    Low cholesterol, lower calorie French cooking.
1. Low-cholesterol diet.   2. Cookery, French.
I. Title. [DNLM: 1. Cholesterol, Dietary—
Popular works. 2. Cookery. WB405 L531L 1974]
RM237.75.L45   641.5′638   73-19288

ISBN 0-684-13745-3

1 3 5 7 9 11 13 15 17 19 C/C 20 18 16 14 12 10 8 6 4 2

Printed in the United States of America

Contents

Introduction

During the past fifty years, the death rate from diseases of the heart and arteries has more than doubled in the United States. Heart attacks alone kill more than half a million Americans each year, many in their prime. Current medical studies indicate that a direct relationship exists between the foods we eat and the incidence of coronary disease. In addition, people who are overweight are more likely to suffer from diseases of the circulatory system than those whose weight is normal.

Many medical men who have studied the connection between health and diet are convinced that a wax-like substance called cholesterol is responsible for the development of many coronary and circulatory ailments. One of these, arteriosclerosis, is a disease in which cholesterol and other fatty substances become embedded in the inner walls of the arteries, narrowing the passages and hampering the rate of blood flow. This narrowing can lead to strokes, heart attacks, and other serious illnesses.

Although diseases of the heart and circulatory system may not manifest themselves until middle age or later they begin to develop early in life, and signs of atherosclerosis have been found in all age groups, including children.

Paradoxically, some cholesterol is essential to good health: it is found throughout the body, including the brain and nerve tissues, helping these to function properly. In excess, however, it is dangerous.

Cholesterol is obtained in two ways: it is manufactured by the body from all foods; and we get it directly by eating foods of animal origin, such as eggs, butter, whole milk, cream, cheeses made from whole milk and cream, and animal fats such as lard. As our standard of living has increased over the past fifty years, so, too, has our consumption of cholesterol-rich foods.

The rate at which the body produces cholesterol is determined to a large extent by the type and quantity of fats in the diet. Saturated fats tend to raise the levels of cholesterol in the blood. Polyunsaturated fats reduce the levels of cholesterol in the blood by helping the body eliminate excesses.

Saturated fats are found in most meats, in dairy products such as butter, whole milk, cream, and cheeses made from whole milk and cream, in some vegetable oils such as palm oil and coconut oil, and in vegetable oils that have been artificially hardened. This hardening, called hydrogenation, is necessary to improve the keeping qualities of some foods, and to make them solid at room temperatures. Many shortenings and margarines, for example, contain hydrogenated vegetable oils. The greater the quantity of hydrogenated oils in a food, the greater are its cholesterol-producing capabilities.

Polyunsaturated fats are found in most vegetable oils, such as corn, cottonseed, safflower, sesame seed, soybean, and sunflower oils. In addition, the oils found in nuts and in grains are high in polyunsaturates, as are most fish oils.

A third category of fats, the monounsaturates, does not raise or lower blood cholesterol levels. Olive and peanut oils belong in this group.

Although it is neither possible nor desirable to eliminate entirely the intake of saturated fats, it is possible to raise the proportion of polyunsaturated to saturated fats by substituting foods containing the former. As the ratio of polyunsaturates to saturated fats increases, the level of cholesterol in the blood decreases correspondingly.

The relationship between fat intake, cholesterol, over-weight, and health has prompted many leading medical authorities to advocate certain basic changes in our eating habits. These include reduced intake of foods containing cholesterol and saturated fats, replacing these with foods containing polyunsaturates, and controlling the number of calories in the diet.

In attempting to achieve these objectives many nutritionists recommend programs that are much more austere than necessary. Actually, it is possible to reduce both cholesterol and caloric intake, yet at the same time continue eating many delicious dishes chosen from among the finest cuisines. French cooking, considered by many to be the best in the world, is a case in point. French cooking is characterized by superb sauces, the imaginative use of wines and the subtle blending of herbs. Even the French dishes made with cheese, butter, eggs, and cream or whole milk can be enjoyed by the individual who is willing to compromise. Much of the original flavor of a Béchamel Sauce, for example, can be retained by substituting corn oil for butter, and skim milk for whole. These two simple steps reduce cholesterol to a minimum and lower the calories without significantly altering the flavor and texture. The same is true of the Brown Sauces, which are delectable even when we replace butter with corn oil.

The recipes in this book have been especially developed to conform with standards of good eating practices as set forth by the American Heart Association. The number of eggs, for example, has been kept to a minimum. Even in such normally high egg dishes as soufflés, the number has been reduced significantly. Recently, a new product called Egg Beaters has reached supermarket shelves. It is an egg substitute which contains practically no cholesterol, yet retains much of the flavor of eggs. For those desiring to reduce cholesterol even further than the low levels in most of the recipes in this book, Egg Beaters can be substituted at the rate of ¼ cup for 1 large egg. However, since the maximum number of eggs in any recipe in this book is one, such substitution is not considered necessary.

Skim milk is an especially healthful food. It contains about half the calories of an equal amount of whole milk, virtually no cholesterol, and essentially the same vitamins and minerals. Whole milk contains about 45 times the amount of fats that skim milk does, and has not been used in any of our recipes.

Extensive use has been made of corn oil because it is flavorful, high in polyunsaturates, and easily available. It is entirely possible that other vegetable oils that are high in polyunsaturates, such as soybean and safflower, are just as good as corn oil, and adventurous cooks can substitute these in some of the recipes and decide for themselves which they prefer. We have had good results with corn oil and are completely satisfied with it.

We have not used margarines in our recipes because all of these, being solid at room temperatures, contain at least some hydrogenated vegetable oil, and we have attempted to keep the ratio of polyunsaturates to saturated fats at a maximum.

The use of artificial sweeteners in lieu of some sugar effectively lowers the calorie content of many of the desserts in this book without affecting flavor. Those interested in cutting calories even further can add additional sugar substitute for sugar, replacing one tablespoon of sugar with one gram of artificial sweetener. To those not primarily interested in reducing calories, sugar substitute can be replaced in all the recipes on the same basis—one tablespoon of sugar for each gram of sweetener.

The use of cheese has been restricted to cottage cheese, which is high in protein, low in cholesterol, and lower in calories than most other cheeses. High cholesterol, high calorie cheeses such as cream, gruyère, etc., have been eliminated along with heavy and light sweet cream.

It has been necessary to omit some favorites because of the nature of their ingredients. It was not possible to develop a tasty Hollandaise Sauce, for example, because the basic ingredient, egg yolks, could not be used. We have kept the use of nuts to a minimum because they are high in calories. Where a recipe includes nuts, we have used just enough to make it tasty.

Each recipe in this book lists the number of calories per serving, the number of grams of saturated and polyunsaturated fats, and the number of milligrams of cholesterol per serving. Calorie and fat values were tabulated from information found in U.S. Department of Agriculture Handbook Number 8, "Composition of Foods." Cholesterol values were obtained from the August, 1972 issue of *The Journal of the American Dietetic Association*; these were tabulated in an article entitled, "Cholesterol Content of Foods," by R. M. Feeley et al. The American Heart Association graciously provided information about cholesterol, fats and hydrogenation.

Over the years we have been discovering, much to our dismay, that many of our favorite foods and activities are potentially hazardous to our health. This book attempts to reverse the trend—the restoration of one of our more pleasurable activities—eating superb French cuisine without harm.

Soups

SOUPE AUX CHOUX
(Cabbage Soup)

> 1 head roughly sliced cabbage
> 8 cups hot water
> 3 beef bouillon cubes
> 2 medium carrots, peeled and sliced
> 1 cup diced celery
> 3 leeks, white part only, sliced
> 1 cup diced turnips
> 3 medium sized potatoes, peeled and sliced
> 1 cup fresh white beans (optional)
> 1 teaspoon salt*
> ¼ teaspoon black pepper
> 2 cloves crushed garlic
> ¼ teaspoon crushed chili peppers
> ¼ teaspoon thyme
> ½ teaspoon chopped parsley

Bring the water to a boil in a large saucepan or soup kettle and stir in the bouillon cubes. Add all other ingredients, and simmer, partially covered, for one hour. Serves 6–8.

* Add more salt to taste, if required.

	WITH BEANS	WITHOUT BEANS
Calories per serving:	130	50
Cholesterol:	5 milligrams	5 milligrams
Saturated fats:	trace	trace
Polyunsaturates:	1 gram	trace

POTAGE AU CHOU-FLEUR
(Cauliflower Soup)

> 1 head medium sized cauliflower
>   OR
> 2 packages frozen cauliflower
> 6 cups lightly salted boiling water
> ¼ cup rice, uncooked
> 1 medium onion, diced
> 2 peeled, sliced medium carrots
> ½ teaspoon salt
> 1 teaspoon chopped parsley
> dash pepper

Add the cauliflower to the water in a large saucepan, cover, and boil until tender. Remove the cauliflower, and to the water add the other ingredients. Simmer partly covered for 35 minutes, strain, and mash the vegetables. Cut the cauliflower into approximately 1-inch squares and add, with the mashed vegetables, to the stock. Heat to boiling, adjust seasoning to taste, and serve. Serves 4–6.

Calories per serving: 50
Cholesterol: none
Saturated fats: none
Polyunsatures: trace

SOUPE À L'AIL
(Garlic Soup)

> 14 cloves peeled, crushed garlic
> 1 ¾ quarts (7 cups) water

>   4 medium potatoes, peeled and sliced
>   1 teaspoon salt*
>   ¼ teaspoon black pepper
>   1 teaspoon chopped parsley
>   1 tablespoon corn oil

Bring the water to a boil in a large saucepan and add all ingredients. Simmer partially covered for 45 minutes. Serve on hard toasted rounds of French bread (See recipe page 117). Serves 4–6.

* Add more salt to taste, if required.

Calories per serving: 105
Cholesterol: none
Saturated fats: trace
Polyunsaturates: 1 gram

POTAGE PARMENTIER

(Leek and Potato Soup)

>   4 leeks, white part only
>   1 tablespoon corn oil
>   1 small carrot
>   2 pounds potatoes
>   1 ¾ quarts (7 cups) hot water
>   2 beef bouillon cubes
>   1 teaspoon salt*
>   ¼ teaspoon pepper
>   ¼ cup skim milk
>   1 teaspoon chopped parsley

Heat the oil in a large saucepan. Dice the leeks and sauté them in the oil until they are a light golden brown.

Peel the vegetables. Slice the carrot, and quarter the potatoes, and add these with the salt, pepper, parsley, bouillon cubes, and water, to the leeks. Bring to a boil, then reduce heat, cover, and simmer for 45 minutes. Using a strainer, separate the liquid from the vegetables. Mash the vegetables, and return the liquid and mashed vegetables to the saucepan. Add the skim milk, heat to boiling, but do not boil, and serve. Serves 6.

* Add more salt to taste, if required.

Calories per serving: 110
Cholesterol: 2 milligrams
Saturated fats: trace
Polyunsaturates: 2 grams

VICHYSSOISE

(Puréed Leek and Potato Soup)

3 leeks, white part only
1 tablespoon corn oil
1 small carrot
2 pounds potatoes
1 ¾ quarts (7 cups) hot water
2 chicken bouillon cubes
1 teaspoon salt*
¼ teaspoon pepper
½ cup skim milk
1 teaspoon chopped parsley

Heat the oil in a large saucepan. Dice the leeks and sauté them in the oil until they are a light golden brown. Peel and slice the carrots and potatoes, and add these with the salt, pepper, parsley, bouillon cubes, and water, to the leeks. Bring to a boil, then reduce heat, cover, and simmer for 45 minutes. Purée the soup in an electric blender, stir in the milk, and chill. Serve cold. Garnish with chopped chives, if desired. Serves 6–8.

* Add more salt to taste, if required.

Calories per serving: 105
Cholesterol: trace
Saturated fats: trace
Polyunsaturates: 1 gram

POTAGE VELOUTÉ AUX CHAMPIGNONS
(Cream of Mushroom Soup)

1 quart boiling water
3 chicken bouillon cubes
8 ounces drained, canned mushrooms, chopped fine
½ teaspoon salt
⅓ cup cooking sherry
¾ cup skim milk

In a medium saucepan dissolve the bouillon cubes in the boiling water, add the salt and mushrooms, cover, and simmer for 25 minutes. Remove from heat, stir in the sherry and milk, blend at high speed for 30 seconds, reheat to boiling but do not boil, and serve. Serves 4.

Calories per serving: 50
Cholesterol: 1 milligram
Saturated fats: trace
Polyunsaturates: trace

SOUPE À L'OIGNON

(Onion Soup)

3 medium onions
2 tablespoons corn oil
¼ teaspoon sugar
¼ teaspoon salt
2 tablespoons all purpose flour
1 ½ quarts boiling water
5 beef bouillon cubes
2 tablespoons dry vermouth
½ teaspoon butter flavor

Peel and slice the onions very thin and cook them slowly with the oil in a heavy saucepan for 15 minutes, stirring frequently. Add the sugar and salt and continue cooking until the onions are an even golden brown. Stir frequently. When the onions are brown, sprinkle in the flour, and when well blended with the onions add the water and the bouillon cubes. Stir gently and add the vermouth and butter flavor. Cover and simmer for 45 minutes, stirring occasionally. Serve in a heated soup tureen or in individual cups. Onion soup can be served plain or on a hard-toasted round of French bread (see page 117) in each cup. Serves 4–6.

Calories per serving: 90
Cholesterol: 9 milligrams
Saturated fats: 1 gram
Polyunsaturates: 3 grams

POTAGE ST. GERMAIN

(Green Pea Soup)

4 cups boiling water
2 chicken bouillon cubes
1 pound canned, drained green peas
1 medium carrot, peeled and sliced
1 medium onion, diced
1 stalk diced celery
½ teaspoon butter flavor
1 cup skim milk
½ teaspoon salt*
pinch pepper

Dissolve the bouillon cubes in the boiling water. Add the vegetables and simmer in a partly covered saucepan for 40 minutes. Strain, mash the vegetables, and return them to the liquid. Place over a small flame and stir in the butter flavor, milk, salt, and pepper. Heat to the boiling point, but do not boil. Serve hot. Serves 4–6.

* Add more salt to taste, if required.

Calories per serving: 80
Cholesterol: trace
Saturated fats: trace
Polyunsaturates: trace

POTAGE MONT ROUGE

(Tomato Soup)

5 medium tomatoes, peeled and sliced
2 medium carrots, peeled and sliced
2 medium potatoes, peeled and sliced
6 cups boiling water
1 teaspoon salt
dash pepper
¼ teaspoon garlic powder

Combine all ingredients in a saucepan, cover, and simmer for one hour. Place in a blender and purée. Heat to boiling, adjust seasoning to taste, and serve. Serves 4–6.

Calories per serving: 70
Cholesterol: none
Saturated fats: none
Polyunsaturates: trace

POTAGE CRÈME DE MONT ROUGE

(Cream of Tomato Soup)

Follow the tomato soup recipe, omitting the pepper and garlic powder. After puréeing, stir in 1 cup skim milk, heat, and serve. Serves 4–6.

Calories per serving: 85
Cholesterol: 1 milligram
Saturated fats: trace
Polyunsaturates: trace

MADRILÈNE

(Jellied Consommé)

>   4 cups hot water
>   2 beef bouillon cubes
>   2 cups tomato juice
>   2 envelopes unflavored gelatin
>   juice of 1 small lemon
>   ½ teaspoon chopped parsley

Dissolve the bouillon cubes in the hot water. Add the tomato juice, gelatin, and lemon juice. Stir until the gelatin is dissolved, then chill thoroughly in the refrigerator. Before serving, beat with a fork and garnish with chopped parsley. Serves 6–8.

Calories per serving: 20
Cholesterol: trace
Saturated fats: trace
Polyunsaturates: trace

POTAGE CULTIVATEUR

(Old Fashioned Vegetable Soup)

>   3 quarts water
>   2 cups diced carrots
>   2 cups diced potatoes
>   1 cup diced onion or leek, white part only
>   1 cup diced celery
>   1 tablespoon salt
>   1 package frozen cut green beans
>   one 16 ounce can navy or kidney beans, drained

one 16 ounce can green peas, drained
¾ cup vermicelli, uncooked, broken into
  approximately 1-inch pieces
¼ teaspoon black pepper
½ teaspoon parsley flakes
4 cloves mashed garlic
¼ teaspoon dried basil

In a large saucepan or soup kettle boil the water and add the salt, carrots, potatoes, onion, and celery. Cover partially and simmer for 45 minutes. Add all other ingredients, cook an additional 15 minutes over low heat, and serve, after adjusting seasoning to taste. Serves 8–10.

Calories per serving: 130
Cholesterol: 10 milligrams
Saturated fats: trace
Polyunsaturates: trace

POTAGE AU CRESSON

(Watercress Soup)

Follow the Potage Parmentier recipe (page 5), adding 1 cup of cleaned, trimmed watercress to the vegetables.

Calories per serving: 115
Cholesterol: 2 milligrams
Saturated fats: trace
Polyunsaturates: 2 grams

SAUCES

Sauces are the heart of French cooking. Although French sauces for meat, fish, poultry, vegetables, salad dressings, etc., number in the hundreds, there are seven basic groups into which most fall. Of these, three contain eggs, cream, and/or butter in large quantities, and will not be included in this book. In the remaining four categories there is a large and varied selection of delectable sauces which are easy to make as well as healthful.

White Sauces

All white sauces are made with a *roux:* corn oil and all-purpose flour cooked together gently until foamy, to eliminate the floury taste. To the *roux* is added either milk or bouillon. With a milk base the sauce is a béchamel. With the bouillon, a velouté. It is from these two basic sauces that most white sauces are made. These can be used with fish, poultry, meat, or vegetables.

SAUCE BÉCHAMEL

(Béchamel Sauce) with poultry, veal, vegetables, fish

> *2 tablespoons corn oil*
> *3 tablespoons all purpose flour*
> *1 ½ cups hot skim milk*
> *salt and white pepper*
> *2 drops butter flavor*

Heat the corn oil in a 1 quart saucepan. Blend in the flour and continue cooking over moderate heat until the mixture becomes foamy. Cook one minute longer, then add the hot skim milk. Stir vigorously with a fork or wire whip and continue cooking until the sauce thickens. Remove from heat and add butter flavor and salt and pepper to taste. Makes about 1 ½ cups of sauce.

> *Calories per serving: 38*
> *Cholesterol: trace*
> *Saturated fats: trace*
> *Polyunsaturates: 1 gram*

SAUCE VELOUTÉ

   (Velouté Sauce) with poultry, vegetables, fish

Follow the béchamel sauce directions (page 15), but substitute 2 chicken bouillon cubes dissolved in 1 ½ cups boiling water for the hot skim milk.

As an alternative, fish stock or the cooking liquids obtained after poaching fish (pages 34, 35) can also be used.

> *Calories per serving: 28*
> *Cholesterol: trace*
> *Saturated fats: trace*
> *Polyunsaturates: 1 gram*

SAUCE AURORE

(Aurora Sauce) with poultry, fish, or vegetables

> *1 ½ cups béchamel or velouté sauce (pages 15, 16)*
> *¼ cup tomato sauce (page 28)*
> *salt and white pepper*

Put the béchamel or velouté sauce in a saucepan over moderate heat and add the tomato sauce a tablespoon at a time until the desired coloring and flavor are obtained. Simmer 1 minute, season to taste. Makes 1 ½ to 2 cups.

> *Calories per serving: 40*
> *Cholesterol: trace*
> *Saturated fats: trace*
> *Polyunsaturates: 1 gram*

SAUCE AUX CÂPRES

(Caper Sauce) with poultry, fish, or veal

> *1 ½ cups béchamel sauce (page 15)*
> *1 tablespoon capers*
> *½ teaspoon parsley flakes*

Combine the sauce and capers in a saucepan over moderate heat and cook until the sauce is hot. Stir in the parsley. Makes about 1 ½ cups.

> *Calories per serving: 40*
> *Cholesterol: Trace*
> *Saturated fats: trace*
> *Polyunsaturates: 1 gram*

SAUCE BÂTARDE
(Substitute Hollandaise Sauce)

2 tablespoons corn oil
3 tablespoons all purpose flour
2 cups hot vegetable stock
1 egg yolk
¼ cup skim milk
1 teaspoon lemon juice
salt and white pepper

Place the oil in a saucepan and heat over a small flame for one minute. Remove from heat and blend in the flour using a rubber scraper or a wooden spoon. When a smooth paste has been formed, gradually add the hot stock and mix until smooth. Heat to boiling and boil one minute. Blend the egg yolk with the skim milk. Stir ½ cup of the hot sauce into the egg mixture. Gradually stir the egg mixture into the remaining hot sauce. Heat over low heat for 1 minute. Stir in the lemon juice, add salt and pepper to taste. Makes about 2 cups. For fish, or vegetables such as artichokes, asparagus, broccoli, cauliflower, etc.

Calories per serving: 20
Cholesterol: 17 milligrams
Saturated fats: trace
Polyunsaturates: 2 grams

SAUCE SOUBISE

(Onion Sauce) with fish

> ½ small onion, diced
> 2 tablespoons corn oil
> 3 tablespoons all purpose flour
> 2 cups skim milk
> 2 drops butter flavor
> salt and white pepper

Heat the corn oil in a two quart saucepan and sprinkle the onion over it. Simmer the onion for 15 minutes, stirring frequently. Add the flour gradually, stirring constantly. When the flour is blended in, cover the skillet and cook one minute over very low heat. Bring the milk to a boil and add it gradually to the onion mixture, stirring as you do so. Add salt and pepper to taste and simmer 15 more minutes, stirring occasionally. Remove from heat and stir in the butter flavor. Strain through a fine sieve. Makes about 2 cups.

Calories per serving: 60
Cholesterol: trace
Saturated fats: trace
Polyunsaturates: 2 grams

SAUCE BERCY

(White Wine Sauce) with fish, poultry, vegetables

> *1 tablespoon corn oil*
> *1 tablespoon diced shallot or green onion*
> *½ cup dry white wine*
> *1 cup béchamel sauce (page 15)*
> *¼ teaspoon parsley flakes*
> *salt and white pepper*

Heat the corn oil in a saucepan and add the shallot. Cook over moderate heat for 2 minutes. Add the wine and continue cooking until the liquid has reduced to about ¼ cup. Add the béchamel sauce, stir well, and cook 2–3 minutes longer. Remove from heat, add parsley, stir, season to taste, and serve. Makes about 1 ¼ cups.

Calories per serving: 60
Cholesterol: trace
Saturated fats: trace
Polyunsaturates: 1 gram

SAUCE AU CARI

(White Curry Sauce) with fish, veal, poultry, vegetables

Follow the sauce soubise recipe (page 19) and stir in 2 tablespoons curry powder before adding the milk.

Calories per serving: 62
Cholesterol: trace
Saturated fats: trace
Polyunsaturates: 2 grams

Brown Sauces

The traditional French brown sauces are difficult to make and time consuming as well. The following basic brown sauce is a tasteful, easy to prepare substitute from which other delicious sauces can be made.

SAUCE BRUNE DE BASE
(Basic Brown Sauce) with poultry, veal, vegetables

> 4 tablespoons corn oil
> 3 tablespoons all purpose flour
> ¼ cup each diced carrots, celery, and onions
> 5 beef bouillon cubes dissolved in 5 cups boiling
>   water
> 3 tablespoons tomato paste
> ¼ teaspoon parsley flakes
> salt and black pepper to taste

Heat the corn oil in a 2 quart saucepan. Add the carrots, celery, and onions, and cook for 10 minutes over low heat. Add the flour, mix well, and continue cooking five minutes more. Stir frequently. Gradually add the bouillon and tomato paste and bring to a boil over moderate heat. Add the parsley, reduce heat to low, and simmer for 45 minutes. Skim off any fat or scum as it forms at the surface. Season to taste. Makes about 5 cups of sauce.

Calories per serving: 35
Cholesterol: negligible
Saturated fats: trace
Polyunsaturates: 2 grams

SAUCE MADÈRE

(Brown Madeira Wine Sauce) with veal dishes

> ½ cup Madeira wine
> 2 cups Basic Brown Sauce (page 21)

Boil the wine rapidly in a 1 quart saucepan until it reduces to about 2–3 tablespoons. Stir in the Brown Sauce, heat, and serve. Makes about 2 cups.

Calories per serving: 45
Cholesterol: negligible
Saturated fats: trace
Polyunsaturates: 2 grams

SAUCE AU PORTO

(Brown Port Wine Sauce) with veal dishes

Follow the Brown Madeira Wine Sauce recipe (above), substituting Port for Madeira wine.

Calories per serving: 45
Cholesterol: negligible
Saturated fats: trace
Polyunsaturates: 2 grams

SAUCE DIABLE

(Hot Brown Sauce) for grilled or broiled chicken

> 1 shallot or green onion, diced
> 2 tablespoons corn oil
> 1 cup dry white wine

1 cup Basic Brown Sauce (page 21)
dash black pepper
dash cayenne pepper
pinch dried chervil
¼ teaspoon parsley flakes

Heat the corn oil in a 1 quart saucepan. Add the shallots
or onions and cook over moderate heat for two minutes.
Add the wine and cook until there is about ½ cup of liquid
left. Stir in the brown sauce and simmer 2–3 minutes.
Remove from heat and stir in the remaining ingredients.
Makes about 1 ½ cups.

Calories per serving: 90
Cholesterol: trace
Saturated fats: trace
Polyunsaturates: 2 grams

SAUCE PIQUANTE

(Brown Sauce with Pickles) with hot leftover veal

1 cup Sauce Diable (page 22)
1 tablespoon chopped gherkin pickles
dash Worcestershire sauce

One minute before removing the Sauce Diable from the
heat stir in the pickles and Worcestershire sauce. Makes
about 1 ¼ cups.

Calories per serving: 95
Cholesterol: trace
Saturated fats: trace
Polyunsaturates: 2 grams

SAUCE ROBERT

(Brown Mustard Sauce) with poultry or meat

> ¼ cup finely chopped onion
> 2 tablespoons corn oil
> 1 tablespoon wine vinegar
> ½ cup dry white wine
> 1 cup Basic Brown Sauce (page 21)
> 1 tablespoon Dijon-type prepared mustard
> ¼ teaspoon parsley flakes
> salt and black pepper

Heat the corn oil in a 1 quart saucepan. Add the onion and cook for about 10 minutes, over low heat, until the onions are soft and have just begun to brown. Add the wine and wine vinegar, turn up the heat, and boil the mixture down to about half of its original volume. Add the brown sauce, reduce heat, and simmer uncovered for 10 minutes. Stir in the mustard and parsley, remove from heat, and season to taste. Makes about 1 ¼ cups.

Calories per serving: 95
Cholesterol: trace
Saturated fats: 1 gram
Polyunsaturates: 5 grams

SAUCE BRUNE À L'ESTRAGON

(Brown Tarragon Sauce) with chicken, veal, or vegetables

> 1 cup dry white wine
> 1 shallot or green onion, minced
> 1 teaspoon dried tarragon
> 2 cups Basic Brown Sauce (page 21)
> ½ teaspoon dried tarragon

Place the first three ingredients in a 1 quart saucepan and cook uncovered over high heat until the liquid is reduced to about 3 tablespoons. Strain into the Brown Sauce, place over moderate heat, and cook for 1 minute. Stir in the ½ teaspoon tarragon, simmer for ½ minute more, and serve. Makes about 2 cups.

> *Calories per serving: 60*
> *Cholesterol: negligible*
> *Saturated fats: trace*
> *Polyunsaturates: 1 gram*

SAUCE BRUNE AUX FINES HERBES

(Brown Herb Sauce) with chicken, veal, or vegetables

Follow the Brown Tarragon Sauce recipe (above), substituting mixed dried parsley, chervil, oregano, and basil for the dried tarragon.

> *Calories per serving: 60*
> *Cholesterol: negligible*
> *Saturated fats: trace*
> *Polyunsaturates: 1 gram*

SAUCE BRUNE AU CARI

(Brown Curry Sauce) with chicken or rice dishes

> 3 tablespoons corn oil
> 1 cup finely chopped onions
> 1 tablespoon curry powder
> 1 clove crushed garlic
> 2 cups Basic Brown Sauce (page 21)
> 1 teaspoon lemon juice
> salt

Heat the oil in a 6- or 8-cup saucepan. Add the onions and cook until they are soft and just turning brown. Stir in the curry powder, and crushed garlic, and cook over moderate heat for one minute. Add the Brown Sauce and reduce heat to low. Cook for 10 minutes. Remove from heat, stir in lemon juice, and season to taste. Makes about 2 ½ cups.

Calories per serving: 70
Cholesterol: negligible
Saturated fats: 1 gram
Polyunsaturates: 3 grams

Other Sauces

SAUCE AUX CHAMPIGNONS

(Mushroom Sauce)

> *½ pound minced fresh mushrooms*
> *3 tablespoons corn oil*
> *2 drops butter flavor*
> *1 cup boiling water*
> *2 beef bouillon cubes*
> *1 tablespoon cornstarch*
> *2 tablespoons cold water*
> *¼ cup Madeira or Port wine*
> *salt and pepper to taste*

Wash, clean, and mince the mushrooms. Heat the corn oil and sauté the mushrooms in a skillet for 5 minutes. Remove from heat, stir in the butter flavor, and set aside. Dissolve the bouillon cubes in the boiling water. Blend the cornstarch and cold water together, and add to the bouillon. Simmer until the liquid begins to thicken. Add the wine and mushrooms and simmer 2–3 minutes longer. Season to taste. Serves 4–6.

Calories per serving: 83
Cholesterol: trace
Saturated fats: 1 gram
Polyunsaturates: 4 grams

SAUCE TOMATE

(Basic Tomato Sauce) with fish, veal

⅓ cup each finely diced carrot, celery, onion
2 cloves crushed garlic
3 tablespoons corn oil
2 tablespoons flour
3 beef bouillon cubes dissolved in 2 cups boiling
    water
2 cups canned tomato purée or 4 cups chopped
    fresh red tomatoes
½ bay leaf
4 black peppercorns
¼ teaspoon sugar
salt
pinch thyme
¼ teaspoon parsley flakes

Heat the corn oil in a large saucepan and add the carrots, onions, celery, and garlic. Cook over moderate heat for ten minutes or until the vegetables just begin to brown. Blend in the flour, reduce heat, and cook for four minutes. Stir often. Add the remaining ingredients, bring to a boil, reduce heat, cover, and simmer for 1½ hours. Strain the sauce through a fine sieve. Makes about 3½ cups.

Calories per serving: 45
Cholesterol: trace
Saturated fats: trace
Polyunsaturates: 2 grams

SAUCE TOMATE AUX CHAMPIGNONS
(Tomato Sauce with Mushrooms) with fish or veal

To two cups Basic Tomato Sauce (page 28) add 1 cup canned sliced mushrooms. Simmer for 5 minutes, season to taste.

Calories per serving: 50
Cholesterol: trace
Saturated fats: trace
Polyunsaturates: 2 grams

SAUCE TOMATE AU VIN
(Tomato Sauce with Sherry Wine) with fish

Stir ⅓ cup dry sherry into 2 cups of Basic Tomato Sauce (page 28). Heat and serve.

Calories per serving: 55
Cholesterol: trace
Saturated fats: trace
Polyunsaturates: 2 grams

SAUCE VINAIGRETTE
(French Dressing)

1 tablespoon wine vinegar
1 tablespoon lemon juice
3 tablespoons olive oil
3 tablespoons corn oil
½ teaspoon salt
pinch dry mustard

> *dash black pepper*
> *1 teaspoon mixed dried herbs, such as parsley,*
>   *thyme, chives, basil, tarragon*

Place all the ingredients in a mixing bowl and beat with a rotary beater until combined, or place ingredients in a screw-top jar and agitate until thoroughly combined.

> *Calories per serving: 90*
> *Cholesterol: none*
> *Saturated fats: 2 grams*
> *Polyunsaturates: 6 grams*

SAUCE RAVIGOTE

(Vinaigrette Sauce with Capers, Onion, and Herbs)
with chicken, fish, and vegetables

> *1 cup Vinaigrette Sauce (page 29)*
> *1 teaspoon chopped capers*
> *1 teaspoon chopped onion*
> *½ teaspoon dried herbs (parsley, chives, chervil,*
>   *tarragon)*

Combine all ingredients and taste for seasoning.

> *Calories per serving: 95*
> *Cholesterol: none*
> *Saturated fats: 2 grams*
> *Polyunsaturates: 6 grams*

Fish and Seafood

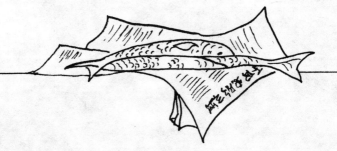

Filet of sole is tasteful, fine-textured, easy to prepare, and versatile. It is little wonder, therefore, that some of the most popular French recipes are those containing this adaptable fish.

True sole is not native to American waters. It is sometimes flown in from Europe, where it is in abundant supply. There are many flatfish in the United States which are comparable in flavor and texture to the European sole and which are very adequate substitutes. The most common types of flatfish available in this country are flounders, some varieties of which are sold as gray or lemon sole. Flounder or other types of flatfish filets can be substituted in any of the following sole recipes with excellent results.

In addition, trout, salmon, and tuna recipes have been included to make the selection of fish recipes a little more varied. Seafood recipes have been limited to clams, mussels, scallops, and frogs' legs because lobster, shrimp, and crabmeat are relatively high in cholesterol.

SOLE GRILLÉE
(Broiled Sole)

> *1 ½ pounds sole filets*
> *salt and black pepper*
> *flour*
> *corn oil*
> *parsley flakes*
> *sliced lemon*

Salt and pepper the sole lightly on both sides, dust with flour and brush with corn oil. Set oven to broil, arrange the sole on a lightly oiled broiling pan, and broil about 5 minutes on each side, or until lightly browned. Sprinkle with parsley and garnish with lemon slices. Serves 4.

Calories per serving: 275
Cholesterol: 75 milligrams
Saturated fats: 2 grams
Polyunsaturates: 9 grams

FILETS DE SOLE POCHÉS

(Filet of Sole Poached in Wine)

¼ cup diced onion
1 diced shallot
1 ½ pounds filet of sole, fresh, or thawed frozen
dry white wine or dry white vermouth
water
salt and white pepper
Sauce (see below)

Sprinkle the onion and shallot over the bottom of a lightly oiled fireproof baking dish. Lay the fish over the onions and season lightly with salt and pepper. Cover the fish with half wine or vermouth and half water and heat on the stove over moderate heat until the liquid begins to simmer. Do not boil. Cover the baking dish with wax paper and move to a pre-heated 325° oven. Bake about 12–15 minutes, or until a fork easily pierces the fish. Drain off the liquid and save it. Serve the fish with Curry or Tarragon Sauce, or with a Velouté (pages 20, 25, 16), using 1½ cups of the liquid in place of the bouillon or fish stock. Serves 4.

Calories per serving: 210
Cholesterol: 75 milligrams
Saturated fats: trace
Polyunsaturates: 1 gram

FILETS DE SOLE AUX CHAMPIGNONS
(Filet of Sole with Mushrooms Poached in Wine)

Follow the Filet of Sole Poached in Wine recipe (page 34), substituting ½ pound sliced fresh cooked or canned mushrooms in place of the onion and shallot.

Calories per serving: 215
Cholesterol: 75 milligrams
Saturated fats: trace
Polyunsaturates: 1 gram

FILETS DE SOLE À LA BOURGUIGNONNE
(Sole Poached in Red Wine)

1 ½ pounds filet of sole
salt and black pepper
Burgundy or other dry red wine
water
1 tablespoon flour
2 tablespoons corn oil
2 drops butter flavor

Lightly salt and pepper the fish and place in a skillet. Cover with two parts wine to one part water. Bring to a simmer, reduce heat, cover, and simmer an additional 8 to 12 minutes, or until a fork easily pierces the flesh. Remove from heat, drain the liquid into a saucepan, and boil it down to approximately 1½ cups. In another saucepan, heat the corn oil, stir in the flour, and cook over moderate heat for 1 minute, stirring constantly. Add the fish liquid to the *roux* and stir vigorously with a fork, slotted spoon, or wire whip until it thickens. Remove from heat and stir in the butter flavor. Season to taste. Drain any residual liquids from the fish, transfer to a serving plate, pour on the wine sauce, and serve. Serves 4.

Calories per serving: 250
Cholesterol: 75 milligrams
Saturated fats: trace
Polyunsaturates: 3 grams

SOLE À LA MEUNIÈRE
(Fried Sole)

1 ½ pounds sole filets
skim milk
flour
corn oil
salt and pepper
parsley flakes
lemon slices

Dip the fish in skim milk, dust both sides with flour and deep fry in corn oil heated to 375° about 4 to 6 minutes or until golden brown. Drain on paper toweling. Sprinkle lightly with parsley flakes, salt and pepper to taste, and garnish with lemon slices. Serves 4.

Calories per serving: 250
Cholesterol: 75 milligrams
Saturated fats: 2 grams
Polyunsaturates: 8 grams

FILETS DE SOLE ORLY
(Deep Fried Sole with Tomato Sauce)

Follow the Sole Meunière recipe (page 36) and serve
with Tomato Sauce (page 28) on the side.

Calories per serving: 295
Cholesterol: 75 milligrams
Saturated fats: 2 grams
Polyunsaturates: 9 grams

FILETS DE SOLE FLORENTINE
(Poached Filet of Sole with Spinach)

1 ½ pounds filet of sole, fresh or thawed frozen
1 chopped shallot
salt and white pepper
dry white wine or vermouth
water
Sauce Velouté (page 16)
1 ½ cups cooked spinach, fresh or frozen

Pre-heat oven to 325°. Lightly salt and pepper the sole
and place, with the shallot, in a fireproof casserole or
baking dish. Cover with a mixture of two-thirds wine and
one-third water, or half vermouth and half water. Place
over moderate heat on the stove and bring to a simmer.
Cover with wax paper and transfer the fish to the center
rack of the oven for approximately 10 minutes, or until a
fork easily pierces the fish. Drain the liquid from the fish
and use 1½ cups to make the Sauce Velouté. Spread the

spinach over the bottom of a serving dish. Place the sole over the spinach, cover with sauce, and serve. Serves 4.

Calories per serving: 230
Cholesterol: 75 milligrams
Saturated fats: trace
Polyunsaturates: 1 gram

FILET DE SOLE PORTUGAISE
(Filet of Sole with Tomatoes, Garlic, and Wine)

1 ½ pounds filet of sole
1 small onion, diced
3 medium tomatoes, quartered
1 clove crushed garlic
2 tablespoons corn oil ⎤
2 tablespoons olive oil ⎦ *mixed together*
½ cup dry white wine
salt and black pepper
parsley flakes

Pre-heat oven to 350°. Place the fish in a lightly oiled baking dish, season with salt and pepper, and sprinkle with two tablespoons of the oil mixture. Put the other two tablespoons of oil in a saucepan, add the onion, garlic, and tomatoes, and cook over moderate heat for 5 minutes, stirring frequently. Add the wine, cook one minute longer, then spoon the mixture over the fish. Bake 20–25 minutes or until a fork easily pierces the fish. Sprinkle with parsley flakes and serve. Serves 4.

Calories per serving: 300
Cholesterol: 75 milligrams
Saturated fats: 2 grams
Polyunsaturates: 8 grams

SAUMON AU SAUCE VELOUTÉ

(Poached Salmon with Velouté Sauce)

> *2 salmon steaks (about 1 ½ pounds)*
> *dry white wine*
> *water*
> *Sauce Velouté (page 16)*
> *salt and black pepper*
> *parsley flakes*

Place the salmon steaks in a large skillet, cover with a mixture of ½ wine and ½ water, bring to a simmer, reduce heat, and continue simmering until a fork easily pierces the salmon, about 8–10 minutes. Drain off the liquid, and use 1 ½ cups to prepare the Velouté Sauce. Place the salmon on a serving dish, cover with sauce, sprinkle with parsley, and serve. Serves 4.

Calories per serving: 390
Cholesterol: 50 milligrams
Saturated fats: 8 grams
Polyunsaturates: 16 grams

SOUFFLÉ DE SAUMON
(Salmon Soufflé)

3 tablespoons corn oil
3 tablespoons all purpose flour
1 teaspoon minced onion
1 cup hot skim milk
1 egg yolk
1 cup cooked or canned salmon, drained and
     shredded
salt and white pepper
pinch oregano or basil
4 egg whites
¼ teaspoon cream of tartar

Pre-heat oven to 375°.

Heat the corn oil in a saucepan and add the flour. Blend thoroughly and stir until the mixture begins to froth. Add the onion and cook for one minute, stirring constantly. Add the milk and stir vigorously with a fork, slotted spoon, or wire whip until the mixture begins to thicken. Add oregano or basil and season to taste with salt and pepper. Remove from heat and beat in the egg yolk. Stir in the salmon. Beat the egg whites until foamy, add the cream of tartar, then beat until stiff. Fold the egg whites into the salmon mixture. Turn into a lightly oiled 1½ quart soufflé mold or baking dish and bake 30–35 minutes, or until the soufflé has risen and the top is golden brown. Serves 4.

Calories per serving: 225
Cholesterol: 63 milligrams
Saturated fats: 3 grams
Polyunsaturates: 9 grams

TRUITE À LA MEUNIÈRE

(Pan Fried Trout)

> 4 dressed trout, about ½ pound each
> ½ cup skim milk
> all purpose flour
> corn oil
> lemon wedges
> salt

Heat the corn oil in a large skillet. Dip the trout in the milk, dust both sides with flour, and fry, browning both sides of the fish. Place on a serving dish, sprinkle with parsley flakes, and serve with lemon wedges. Salt to taste. Serves 4.

> *Calories per serving: 100*
> *Cholesterol: 60 milligrams*
> *Saturated fats: 2 grams*
> *Polyunsaturates: 6 grams*

THON GRILLÉ

(Grilled Tuna)

> 4 tuna steaks, about ½ pound each
> salt and black pepper
> corn oil
> parsley flakes
> lemon wedges

Sprinkle both sides of the fish with salt and pepper, brush with corn oil, place in a lightly oiled broiling pan, and broil 5 minutes. Turn the fish carefully and broil another 5 minutes, or until a fork easily pierces the fish. Sprinkle with parsley flakes and serve with lemon wedges. Serves 4.

Calories per serving: 360
Cholesterol: 75 milligrams
Saturated fats: 3 grams
Polyunsaturates: 8 grams

SOUFFLÉ DE THON
(Tuna Soufflé)

Follow the salmon soufflé recipe, substituting 1 cup flaked or shredded tuna fish, cooked fresh or canned, for the salmon. Serves 4.

Calories per serving: 20
Cholesterol: 63 milligrams
Saturated fats: 3 grams
Polyunsaturates: 9 grams

SOUFFLÉ DE POISSON
(Fish Soufflé)

  1 tablespoon corn oil
  1 tablespoon diced onion
  ½ pound skinless flounder, cod, haddock, or
    halibut filets, fresh or frozen (defrosted)
  ¼ teaspoon salt

dash black pepper
⅓ cup dry white wine or dry vermouth
2 tablespoons corn oil
3 tablespoons all purpose flour
1 cup hot skim milk
1 egg yolk
4 egg whites
¼ teaspoon cream of tartar
salt and black pepper to taste

Pre-heat oven to 375°.

Heat one tablespoon oil in a saucepan, add the onion, and place the fish filets in it. Sprinkle with salt and pepper, add the wine or vermouth, cover, and cook over moderate heat until a fork pierces the fish easily, about 15 minutes. Chop the fish fine or force it through a fine sieve, or purée it in a blender. In another saucepan heat 2 tablespoons corn oil, blend in the flour, and cook until the mixture begins to froth. Stir constantly and cook one more minute. Add the hot milk, continue cooking and stirring until the sauce beings to thicken. Use a wire whip, slotted spoon, or fork to stir. Remove from heat, add the fish, stir, add salt and pepper to taste. Beat in the egg yolk. Beat the egg whites until foamy. Add the cream of tartar and beat until stiff. Carefully fold the egg whites into the fish mixture. Spoon the mixture carefully into a lightly oiled 1½ quart soufflé mold or baking dish and bake for approximately 30 minutes, or until the soufflé has risen and the top is golden brown. Serves 4.

Calories per serving: 240
Cholesterol: 63 milligrams
Saturated fats: 2 grams
Polyunsaturates: 7 grams

CLAMS À LA MARINIÈRE
(Steamed Clams)

> 4 quarts soft shell steamer clams (Be certain the
>   shells are closed tightly)
> 2 cups boiling water
> 1 teaspoon lemon juice
> 2 drops butter flavor

Wash the clams under cold running water to remove as much sand as possible. Put the boiling water in a large kettle, add the clams, cover, and steam until the shells open, about 5 to 10 minutes. Strain the broth through several thicknesses of cheesecloth, add the lemon juice and butter flavor, stir, and serve in cups. Put the clams in soup plates and serve with oyster forks. The clams are removed from the shell with the oyster fork, dipped in the broth, and eaten. Provide a large dish for discarded shells. Serves 4.

Calories per serving: 250
Cholesterol: 72 milligrams
Saturated fats: 1 gram
Polyunsaturates: 3 grams

CLAMS À LA CRÉOLE
(Clams Creole)

> 2 cups raw hard shell clams, shucked, cleaned, and
>   drained
> 1 cup dry white wine
> 1 small onion, diced
> 1 tablespoon corn oil
> ¼ teaspoon curry powder
> 2 cups cooked rice

salt and black pepper
lemon wedges

Combine the wine, onion, corn oil, and curry powder in
a saucepan, bring to a boil over moderate heat, reduce
heat, and simmer for 2 minutes. Add the clams, cover, and
cook 3 minutes longer. Put the rice in a serving dish, place
the clams over them, pour the liquid over the clams,
season to taste, garnish with lemon wedges, and serve.
Serves 4.

Calories per serving: 350
Cholesterol: 72 milligrams
Saturated fats: 2 grams
Polyunsaturates: 5 grams

MOULES À LA CRÉOLE
(Mussels Creole)

Substitute raw shucked mussels for the clams in the
Clams à la Créole recipe.

Calories per serving: 355
Cholesterol: 70 milligrams
Saturated fats: 2 grams
Polyunsaturates: 5 grams

MOULES À LA MARINIÈRE
(Steamed Mussels)

4 quarts mussels
1 ½ cups water
½ cup dry white wine } *boiled together*
pinch of parsley flakes
dash black pepper

Wash the mussels in cold running water to remove as much sand as possible. Put the boiling liquid in a large kettle with the parsley flakes and black pepper, add the mussels, cover, and steam until the shells open, about 5–10 minutes. Strain the broth through several thicknesses of cheesecloth, and set aside. Serve the mussels in soup plates, providing a separate dish for discarded shells. Just before serving, boil the broth and pour it over the mussels, which are removed from their shells with an oyster fork. Serves 4.

Calories per serving: 275
Cholesterol: 70 milligrams
Saturated fats: 1 gram
Polyunsaturates: 3 grams

COQUILLES ST. JACQUES
(Scallops in Wine)

1 cup dry white wine
1 pound washed and drained fresh scallops
pinch salt, dash pepper
½ pound sliced mushrooms, cooked fresh or canned
3 finely chopped shallots or ½ small chopped onion
1 teaspoon finely chopped parsley
1 teaspoon corn oil
1 teaspoon lemon juice
3 tablespoons water
2 tablespoons all purpose flour

2 tablespoons corn oil
¼ teaspoon butter flavor
¼ cup skim milk

Bring the wine to a boil in a saucepan. Add the salt, pepper, and scallops, and simmer for 5 minutes. Drain the scallops, setting aside the liquid. Cut the scallops crosswise in fine pieces about one eighth inch thick. Combine the mushrooms, shallots, parsley, teaspoon corn oil, lemon juice, and water in a saucepan and simmer for 10 minutes. Drain and add the liquid to the wine sauce. In another saucepan combine the 2 tablespoons corn oil with the flour and stir constantly over low heat until the ingredients are blended. Add the liquid from the scallops and mushrooms gradually to the flour mixture, stirring constantly until it is smooth and has begun to thicken. Add the skim milk, and butter flavor, remove from heat, and stir in the mushrooms and scallops. Place the scallops and sauce in scallop shells and brown several minutes under the broiler flame. Serves 4.

Calories per serving: 270
Cholesterol: 44 milligrams
Saturated fats: 1 gram
Polyunsaturates: 6 grams

COQUILLES ST. JACQUES AU DIABLE

(Deviled Scallops)

2 pounds bay scallops
1 medium onion, diced
6 tablespoons corn oil
3 tablespoons all purpose flour
¼ cup dry white wine
½ teaspoon Dijon-type prepared mustard
½ teaspoon salt
dash Cayenne pepper
¼ teaspoon parsley flakes
1 cup soft breadcrumbs

Pre-heat oven to 350°.

Wash the scallops under cold running water. Drain thoroughly and chop finely. Combine the scallops, onion, and 4 tablespoons corn oil in a saucepan and cook 3 minutes over moderate heat, stirring frequently. Add all other ingredients, except 2 tablespoons corn oil and the breadcrumbs. Cook until the mixture thickens, then remove from heat. Spoon the mixture into a lightly oiled casserole, then mix the breadcrumbs and remaining corn oil together and cover the scallops. Bake uncovered until the breadcrumbs are brown, about 20–25 minutes. Serves 6.

Calories per serving: 320
Cholesterol: 59 milligrams
Saturated fats: 2 grams
Polyunsaturates: 9 grams

COQUILLES ST. JACQUES AUX CHAMPIGNONS

(Scallops with Mushrooms in Wine Sauce)

> 2 pounds bay scallops
> 1 small white onion, diced
> ¼ teaspoon parsley flakes
> dry white wine
> ½ cup sliced mushrooms, cooked fresh or canned
> 5 tablespoons corn oil
> ¼ cup hot water
> 2 tablespoons flour
> ¾ cup breadcrumbs
> salt and black pepper

Wash the scallops under cold running water. Place them with the onion and parsley flakes in a saucepan and add enough white wine to cover. Bring to a simmer, reduce heat, and continue simmering until tender, about 8 minutes. Drain and set aside the liquid. Heat 3 tablespoons corn oil in a large saucepan, blend in the flour, cook 1 minute over moderate heat, stirring constantly. Stir in the scallop liquid and mix vigorously with a fork, slotted spoon, or wire whisk until the mixture thickens smoothly. Remove from heat. Add salt and pepper to taste. Add the mushrooms and scallops. Mix gently, then spoon the mixture into lightly oiled individual scallop shells or a casserole. Mix 2 tablespoons corn oil with the bread crumbs, sprinkle over the scallops, and broil until the crumbs brown. Serves 6.

Calories per serving: 310
Cholesterol: 60 milligrams
Saturated fats: 2 grams
Polyunsaturates: 7 grams

COQUILLES ST. JACQUES À LA DUCHESSE

(Scallops with Mashed Potatoes)

Follow the Scallops with Mushrooms in Wine Sauce recipe (page 49). Fill 6 lightly oiled scallop shells with the mixture. Mash 2 cups of cooked boiled potatoes with 1 tablespoon corn oil, and add salt and pepper to taste. Place the potatoes in a pastry bag and garnish each shell with a border of potatoes. Broil until brown. Serves 6.

Calories per serving: 375
Cholesterol: 60 milligrams
Saturated fats: 3 grams
Polyunsaturates: 8 grams

GRENOUILLES DU GOURMET PROVENÇALE

(Frogs Legs Sautéed with Garlic)

24 pairs frogs legs
¼ cup corn oil
6 cloves crushed garlic
salt and pepper
parsley flakes
lemon juice

Heat the corn oil in a large skillet. Lightly brown the garlic, then sauté the frogs' legs until they are golden brown on both sides. Arrange on a serving dish, sprinkle with the lemon juice and parsley flakes, and serve. Serves 4–6.

Calories per serving: 200
Cholesterol: 75 milligrams
Saturated fats: 1 gram
Polyunsaturates: 5 grams

Poultry

Chicken is the most popular poultry in the world. It is tasty, readily available, and relatively inexpensive. In addition, it is high in protein and low in fats and calories. It is the most versatile of all poultry, and can be baked, boiled, broiled, sautéed, and fried, with excellent results. Removing the skin before cooking will further reduce calories as well as saturated fats.

Although duck and goose play a prominent role in French cookery, they have been omitted from these pages because of their high fat content.

COQ AU VIN
(Chicken in Red Wine)

> *3 pound frying chicken cut into serving portions*
> *1 cup all purpose flour*
> *3 tablespoons corn oil*
> *salt and white pepper*
> *3 tablespoons cognac*
> *3 cups red wine, such as Burgundy, Chianti, or*
> *Beaujolais*
> *8 small onions*
> *2 tablespoons corn oil*
> *½ pound mushrooms, peeled and sliced, fresh or*
> *canned*
> *chicken stock or bouillon*

Roll the pieces of chicken in the flour and sauté them in large skillet with 3 tablespoons of heated corn oil. Brown the chicken on all sides. Season with salt and pepper, sprinkle the cognac over it, and with your face averted, ignite the cognac. When the flames subside, pour the wine into the skillet. Add just enough stock or bouillon to cover the chicken, cover, and simmer until the chicken is tender, about 30–35 minutes. While the chicken is simmering in the wine, sauté the onions in the 2 tablespoons of corn oil until they are brown. Add the mushrooms and cook until onions and mushrooms are tender. Arrange the vegetables on a platter, place the chicken over them, spoon the wine sauce over the chicken, and serve. Serves 4.

Calories per serving: 780
Cholesterol: 135 milligrams
Saturated fats: 5 grams
Polyunsaturates: 15 grams

POULET RÔTI

(Roast Chicken)

> 3 to 3 ½ pound roasting chicken
> salt and black pepper
> corn oil

Pre-heat oven to 325°. Rub the skin with corn oil, sprinkle with salt and pepper, and place breast side up on a rack in a roasting pan. Roast until tender. The bird is done when the drumstick moves easily. As a further test, prick the drumstick with a fork. The juices should run clear yellow. A 3 pound chicken will require 2½ to 3 hours to cook. Allow ¾ pound per person. Serves 4.

Calories per serving: 330
Cholesterol: 136 milligrams
Saturated fats: 3 grams
Polyunsaturates: 7 grams

POULET SAUTÉ

(Sautéed Chicken)

> 3 to 3 ½ pound cut-up frying chicken
> salt and black pepper
> corn oil
> parsley flakes, dried tarragon, and basil

Dry the chicken thoroughly and rub with salt and pepper. Heat 2–3 tablespoons corn oil in a skillet and place pieces of chicken, skin side down, in a single layer. Cook until brown, then turn until the other side browns. Add corn oil as required to brown all the chicken. After browning, season with herbs, place in the skillet, cover, and cook over moderate heat about 25 minutes, or until tender. Baste 2 or 3 times with the liquid from the skillet. Serves 4.

Calories per serving: 360
Cholesterol: 136 milligrams
Saturated fats: 4 grams
Polyunsaturates: 9 grams

POULET SAUTÉ À LA PORTUGAISE

(Chicken Sautéed with Mushrooms and Tomatoes)

> 3 to 3 ½ pound cut-up frying chicken
> salt and black pepper
> corn oil
> ½ cup dry white wine
> 1 cup sliced mushrooms, canned or fresh
> 1 small diced onion
> 2 medium tomatoes, quartered
> parsley flakes

Pre-heat oven to 350°. Rub the chicken with corn oil, season with salt and pepper, and place in a lightly oiled roasting pan or baking dish. Pour the wine over the chicken and place in the oven. Sauté the mushrooms and onion in 2 tablespoons of corn oil, add the tomatoes, and cook 5 minutes over low heat. When the chicken has been cooking 45 minutes, cover with the mushrooms and tomato mixture and cook 15 minutes longer, or until the chicken is tender. Baste twice. Sprinkle with parsley. Serves 4.

Calories per serving: 385
Cholesterol: 135 milligrams
Saturated fats: 3 grams
Polyunsaturates: 7 grams

POULET SAUTÉ À L'INDIENNE

(Curried Chicken)

3 to 3 ½ pound cut-up frying chicken
1 chopped onion
1 thinly sliced carrot
1 clove crushed garlic
2 tablespoons corn oil ⎫ *mixed together*
2 tablespoons olive oil ⎭
1 tablespoon curry powder
salt and white pepper
3 tablespoons all purpose flour
*4 chicken bouillon cubes dissolved in 4 cups boiling
      water*
½ cup dry white wine
parsley flakes

Heat the oil in a 10-inch skillet or electric skillet to approximately 275°. Add the onion, carrot, and garlic and cook 5 minutes. Add the chicken and cook 5 minutes, turning it frequently to avoid browning. Stir in the curry powder. Lower heat, cover, and cook 10 minutes more. Season with salt and pepper, then sprinkle on the flour, covering all sides of the chicken. Cover and cook an additional 5 minutes. Remove from heat, add the wine and enough bouillon to cover, bring to a simmer, cover, and simmer for 25 minutes more, or until the chicken is tender. Serves 4.

Calories per serving: 490
Cholesterol: 135 milligrams
Saturated fats: 4 grams
Polyunsaturates: 13 grams

POULET SAUTÉ À L'ANCIENNE
(Sautéed Chicken with Wine, Vegetables, and Garlic)

Follow the curried chicken recipe (page 56), but omit the curry powder.

Calories per serving: 485
Cholesterol: 135 milligrams
Saturated fats: 4 grams
Polyunsaturates: 13 grams

FRICASSÉE DE POULET
(Chicken Fricassee)

> *3 pound cut-up frying chicken*
> *salt and black pepper*
> *all purpose flour*
> *corn oil*
> *½ cup dry white wine*
> *3 chicken bouillon cubes dissolved in 2 cups boiling*
> *   water*
> *12 small white onions*
> *1 cup sliced canned mushrooms*
> *¼ teaspoon parsley flakes*

Sprinkle the chicken with salt and pepper and dredge in flour. Heat about 4 tablespoons of corn oil in a heavy skillet or electric skillet and brown the chicken lightly on both sides, adding corn oil as needed. Remove from heat and add the wine, bouillon, onions; cover and cook 30 minutes over low to moderate heat. Stir in the mushrooms, cover, and simmer 10 minutes more, or until the chicken is tender. Sprinkle with parsley flakes. Serves 4.

Calories per serving: 530
Cholesterol: 135 milligrams
Saturated fats: 4 grams
Polyunsaturates: 13 grams

POULETS GRILLÉS
(Broiled Chicken)

> *2 small broilers, about 2 pounds each, halved*
> *corn oil*
> *4 tablespoons prepared Dijon-type mustard*
> *1 medium onion, diced*
> *salt and black pepper*
> *½ teaspoon basil*
> *dash cayenne pepper*

Dry the chicken, brush with corn oil, salt and pepper lightly, and place in a broiling pan. Place the chicken 4–6 inches from the heat and broil 10 minutes on each side. While the chicken is broiling, blend the mustard, onion, and seasonings in a bowl. Remove the chicken from the oven, drain and reserve the drippings; place the chicken on a rack in the broiling pan, skin-side up, brush with oil, and sprinkle the mustard mixture over the chicken. Broil ten minutes under moderate heat, basting with the drippings which were set aside. Turn the chicken and broil ten minutes longer, basting as before, or until the chicken is tender. Serves 4.

Calories per serving: 425
Cholesterol: 150 milligrams
Saturated fats: 4 grams
Polyunsaturates: 10 grams

POULET MARENGO
(Chicken in Wine with Tomatoes)

> *3 pound cut-up frying chicken*
> *salt and black pepper*
> *flour*
> *¼ cup corn oil*
> *1 medium onion, diced*
> *½ cup dry white wine*
> *3 medium tomatoes, quartered*
> *1 clove crushed garlic*
> *parsley flakes*
> *1 cup canned button mushrooms*

Season the chicken lightly with salt and pepper and dredge in flour. Heat the corn oil in a skillet or electric skillet (360°). Brown the chicken lightly on both sides. When the chicken has browned, add the onion, wine, garlic, and parsley. Reduce heat to 300°, add tomatoes, cover, and cook 20 minutes. Add the mushrooms and cook 5 minutes longer, or until the chicken is tender. Season to taste. Serves 4.

> *Calories per serving: 475*
> *Cholesterol: 135 milligrams*
> *Saturated fats: 4 grams*
> *Polyunsaturates: 10 grams*

POULET AU RIZ
(Boiled Chicken with Rice)

> 3 pound chicken, whole
> 2 carrots, sliced
> 1 stalk celery, sliced
> 2 onions, sliced
> 2 leeks, sliced
> salt and black pepper
> 5 chicken bouillon cubes dissolved in 5 cups boiling
>   water
> 1 cup uncooked white rice
> ¼ cup corn oil
> 1 tablespoon cornstarch ⎤
> 1 tablespoon cold water ⎦ mixed together

In a large saucepan bring to a boil 2 cups of the bouillon. Add the chicken and vegetables, ½ teaspoon salt and a dash of black pepper, cover, and simmer 1½ hours, or until tender. In the meantime, soak the rice in cold water for half an hour. When the chicken is done, transfer it to a warm platter and cover. Strain the liquid into a saucepan and add enough bouillon to make 3 cups. Set the vegetables aside. Drain the rice and add it to the bouillon and strained vegetable liquid. Add ½ teaspoon salt, cover, and simmer until the rice is tender, about 15 minutes. Strain and put the rice in a large serving dish. Put the chicken over it, and garnish with the vegetables. Blend the cornstarch/cold water mixture into 1 cup of hot bouillon, bring to a boil, cook 2 minutes, season to taste, and spoon over the chicken. Serves about 4.

Calories per serving: 650
Cholesterol: 135 milligrams
Saturated fats: 4 grams
Polyunsaturates: 13 grams

SUPRÊMES DE VOLAILLE AU VIN

(Chicken Cutlets in Wine Sauce)

4 boned breasts from 2 fryers
salt and pepper
1 cup all purpose flour
½ cup corn oil
1 small onion, diced
¼ cup Port or Madeira wine
2 beef bouillon cubes dissolved in 1 cup boiling
    water
¼ teaspoon parsley flakes

Sprinkle the cutlets with salt and pepper and dredge them in flour. Heat the corn oil in a skillet and sauté the cutlets, giving them about 3 minutes on a side. They are done when a fork easily pierces the flesh and they are springy to the touch. Remove the cutlets from the skillet and set them aside. Add the diced onion, and sauté it for 2 minutes. Add the wine and bouillon and bring to a rapid boil. Continue boiling until the liquid is down to half its original volume. Pour over the cutlets, sprinkle with parsley, and serve. Serves 4.

Calories per serving: 650
Cholesterol: 125 milligrams
Saturated fats: 3 grams
Polyunsaturates: 9 grams

SUPRÊMES DE VOLAILLE AUX CHAMPIGNONS

(Chicken Cutlets in Mushroom Sauce)

Follow the Chicken Cutlets in Wine recipe (page 62), adding ½ cup canned button mushrooms to the wine sauce after it has boiled down. Cook ½ minute over moderate heat before pouring over the cutlets.

Calories per serving: 660
Cholesterol: 125 milligrams
Saturated fats: 3 grams
Polyunsaturates: 9 grams

SOUFFLÉ DE POULET

(Chicken Soufflé)

Follow the salmon soufflé recipe (page 40), substituting 1 cup ground cooked white meat chicken for the salmon. Serves 4.

Calories per serving: 215
Cholesterol: 63 milligrams
Saturated fats: 3 grams
Polyunsaturates: 9 grams

SOUFFLÉ DE DINDON

(Turkey Soufflé)

Follow the salmon soufflé recipe (page 40), substituting 1 cup ground cooked light turkey for the salmon. Serves 4.

Calories per serving: 215
Cholesterol: 63 milligrams
Saturated fats: 3 grams
Polyunsaturates: 9 grams

DINDON RÔTI

(Roast Turkey)

Pre-heat oven to 325°. Brush the bird lightly with corn oil, and sprinkle with salt and pepper. Place the turkey, breast side up, on a rack in a roasting pan and cook until the turkey is done. Baste every half hour with drippings from the pan. Allow about ½ hour per pound for birds up to 10 pounds, 25 minutes per pound for larger turkeys. The bird is done if the juices run clear when the thigh has been pierced with a fork.

Calories per serving: 460
Cholesterol: 150 milligrams
Saturated fats: 6 grams
Polyunsaturates: 15 grams

Poultry Stuffings

The following recipes will stuff a ten pound turkey. For larger or smaller birds modify the recipe proportionately. A stuffed bird will take longer to cook than one that has not been stuffed. Allow 30 minutes longer for a ten pound turkey, about 15 minutes longer for a medium chicken.

FARCIE DE PAIN
(Bread Stuffing)

> 1 medium onion, diced
> 1 stalk celery, chopped fine
> ½ cup corn oil
> 8 cups bread crumbs
>   *(make the crumbs in an electric blender)*
> ½ teaspoon ground sage
> 1 clove crushed garlic
> 1 teaspoon salt
> ¼ teaspoon parsley flakes
> ¼ teaspoon black pepper
> 2 chicken bouillon cubes dissolved in 1 cup boiling
>   water

Heat 2 tablespoons corn oil in a large saucepan and cook the onion and celery for 10 minutes. Add the remaining corn oil, then stir in the remaining ingredients. Remove from heat, stuff and truss the bird, and roast in accordance with instructions.

Calories per serving: 310
Cholesterol: trace
Saturated fats: 2 grams
Polyunsaturates: 8 grams

FARCIE DUXELLES

(Mushroom Stuffing)

Add 1 cup of canned button mushrooms to the Bread Stuffing recipe (page 65).

Calories per serving: 315
Cholesterol: trace
Saturated fats: 2 grams
Polyunsaturates: 8 grams

MEAT

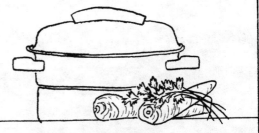

The only meat included in this chapter is veal. Although some low cholesterol cookbooks include beef, lamb, and even pork recipes, these are all high in cholesterol and have no place in a book of this nature.

Veal is especially desirable in low cholesterol cooking because the flesh is not marbled with fat as it is with beef. Veal is obtained from calves 3 months old or younger. It has a delicate flavor, good texture, and the different cuts lend themselves to many excellent recipes.

ESCALOPES DE VEAU VIENNOISE
(Veal Cutlets, Viennese Style)

> *6 veal scallops, about 5–6 ounces each*
> *salt and black pepper*
> *¼ cup corn oil*
> *3 tablespoons breadcrumbs*
> *2 tablespoons all purpose flour*
> *1 egg, well beaten*
> *lemon slices*

Veal scallops are boneless slices of veal cut about ⅜ inches thick and pounded to a thickness of ¼ inch with a wooden mallet or a cleaver. Season the scallops with salt and pepper. Stir together the flour and bread crumbs, dip the scallops in the egg, roll them in the flour/bread mixture, and set aside. Heat the corn oil in a large skillet and brown the scallops over moderate heat on both sides. 4–5 minutes per side should be sufficient. Do not overcook. Season to taste, top with lemon slices, and serve. Serves 4.

Calories per serving: 595
Cholesterol: 283 milligrams
Saturated fats: 9 grams
Polyunsaturates: 15 grams

ESCALOPES DE VEAU CHASSEUR
(Veal Scallops Sautéed with Mushrooms and Tomatoes)

6 veal scallops, pounded very thin
salt and black pepper
3 tablespoons corn oil
2 shallots or ½ small white onion, minced
4 ripe red tomatoes, quartered
1 clove crushed garlic
¼ teaspoon basil or tarragon
½ cup dry white wine
1 beef bouillon cube dissolved in ¾ cup boiling
*   water*
½ cup canned button mushrooms
1 tablespoon cold water ⎱ *mixed together*
1 tablespoon cornstarch ⎰
parsley flakes

Heat the corn oil in a large skillet. Wash and pat the scallops dry on paper towels. Sprinkle with salt and pepper, and sauté 4 to 5 minutes on each side, over moderate heat, until lightly browned. Set the meat aside and in the same skillet add the shallots or onion and cook until they soften. Add the tomatoes, garlic, and herbs, cover, and cook 5 minutes. Add the wine and bouillon and bring to a boil. Stir in the cornstarch mixture. Cook until the mixture begins to thicken. Add the mushrooms, then return the veal to the skillet. Cover and cook over moderate heat about 4 minutes. Sprinkle with parsley. Serves 4.

Calories per serving: 445
Cholesterol: 140 milligrams
Saturated fats: 9 grams
Polyunsaturates: 17 grams

ESCALOPES DE VEAU À L'ANGLAISE
(Breaded Veal Scallops)

6 veal scallops, pounded thin
salt and black pepper
all purpose flour
2 egg whites
corn oil
fine breadcrumbs
lemon slices

Sprinkle the scallops with salt and pepper, roll them in flour, and set aside. Beat the egg whites with one tablespoon of corn oil, dip the veal in this mixture, then dredge in the bread crumbs. Heat 3 tablespoons corn oil in a large skillet and sauté the scallops about 4–5 minutes on each side, or until golden brown. Season to taste, garnish with lemon slices, and serve. Serves 4.

Calories per serving: 400
Cholesterol: 140 milligrams
Saturated fats: 8 grams
Polyunsaturates: 10 grams

ESCALOPES DE VEAU À L'ESTRAGON
(Veal Scallops with Tarragon Sauce)

8 veal scallops, 4–5 ounces each
3 tablespoons corn oil
1 medium onion, or 3 shallots, minced
½ cup dry white wine
2 teaspoons dried tarragon
2 beef bouillon cubes dissolved in 1 cup hot water
1 tablespoon cornstarch ⎫
1 tablespoon cold water ⎭ mixed together
salt and pepper
parsley flakes

Pound the scallops to a thickness of ¼ inch with a wooden mallet or cleaver. Pat dry with paper toweling. Heat the corn oil in a large skillet and sauté the scallops 4–5 minutes on each side over moderate heat. Remove from the skillet to a platter. Sauté the onion or shallots in the same skillet over a low flame until they soften. Add the wine and tarragon and boil down to about 3 tablespoons. Add the bouillon and stir in the cornstarch/water mixture. Cook about 3 minutes, or until the sauce begins to thicken. Return the veal to the skillet, baste with sauce, cover, and simmer until tender, about 5 minutes. Season to taste, sprinkle with parsley, and serve. Serves 4–6.

Calories per serving: 490
Cholesterol: 175 milligrams
Saturated fats: 7 grams
Polyunsaturates: 11 grams

CÔTELETTES DE VEAU EN COCOTTE AU LAIT
(Veal Cutlets in Milk)

4 veal cutlets
2 tablespoons corn oil
salt and black pepper
½ cup skim milk
parsley flakes

Heat the corn oil in a skillet. Wash and pat the cutlets dry. Sprinkle with salt and pepper and brown them lightly on both sides over moderate heat. Add the milk and bring to a simmer. Reduce heat and simmer until the veal is tender, about ten minutes. Season to taste, sprinkle with parsley, and serve. Serves 4.

Calories per serving: 425
Cholesterol: 175 milligrams
Saturated fats: 6 grams
Polyunsaturates: 9 grams

CÔTELETTES DE VEAU GRILLÉES
(Grilled Veal Cutlets)

> *4 veal cutlets*
> *¼ cup corn oil*
> *salt and black pepper*
> *all purpose flour*

Heat the corn oil in a large skillet. Season the cutlets lightly with salt and pepper, dredge in flour, and brown on both sides over moderate heat until tender. Serves 4.

> *Calories per serving: 485*
> *Cholesterol: 175 milligrams*
> *Saturated fats: 7 grams*
> *Polyunsaturates: 13 grams*

CÔTELETTES DE VEAU AUX HERBES
(Veal Cutlets with Herbs)

> *4 veal cutlets*
> *2 tablespoons corn oil*
> *salt and black pepper*
> *all purpose flour*
> *¼ teaspoon each, parsley flakes, basil, and thyme*

Blend together the herbs and flour. Heat the corn oil in a large skillet. Sprinkle the cutlets with salt and pepper, dredge in the herb/flour mixture, and brown on both sides over moderate heat until tender. Season to taste. Serves 4.

> *Calories per serving: 425*
> *Cholesterol: 175 milligrams*
> *Saturated fats: 6 grams*
> *Polyunsaturates: 9 grams*

CÔTELETTES DE VEAU BONNE FEMME
(Veal Cutlets Sautéed with Vegetables)

4 veal cutlets
¼ cup corn oil
8 small white onions
8 ounces canned button mushrooms, drained
6 medium potatoes, peeled and quartered
salt and black pepper
all purpose flour
1 beef bouillon cube dissolved in ½ cup boiling
      water

Pre-heat oven to 325°.

Heat 2 tablespoons corn oil in a skillet. Add the mushrooms and onions and sauté for 5 minutes. Transfer the vegetables to a casserole or baking dish. Add the remaining corn oil to the skillet, heat, then brown the potatoes and put them in the casserole. Sprinkle the cutlets with salt and pepper, dredge in flour and brown in the skillet. Add a little more corn oil if required. Place the cutlets over the vegetables, pour the bouillon over them, cover, and place in oven and cook until the veal is tender, about 30 minutes. Serves 4.

Calories per serving: 660
Cholesterol: 175 milligrams
Saturated fats: 7 grams
Polyunsaturates: 13 grams

CÔTELETTES DE VEAU À LA MÉNAGÈRE (I)

(Veal Cutlets with Browned Vegetables)

> 4 veal cutlets
> salt and black pepper
> ⅓ cup corn oil
> 8 small white onions
> 4 carrots, sliced
> 4 medium potatoes, peeled and sliced
> 2 beef bouillon cubes dissolved in 1 cup boiling
>   water

Heat 2 tablespoons corn oil in a large skillet. Season the cutlets lightly with salt and pepper, then brown on both sides over moderate heat in the oil. Heat the remaining corn oil in a second skillet, add all the vegetables, and brown them. Add the vegetables to the veal, pour in the bouillon, cover, and cook over low heat until the veal is tender, about 35 minutes. Season to taste. Serves 4.

Calories per serving: 660
Cholesterol: 175 milligrams
Saturated fats: 8 grams
Polyunsaturates: 15 grams

CÔTELETTES DE VEAU À LA MÉNAGÈRE (II)
(Veal Cutlets with Browned Vegetables in Wine)

Follow the Veal Cutlets with Browned Vegetables recipe (page 76), but substitute ¾ cup dry white wine and ¼ cup water for the bouillon.

Calories per serving: 685
Cholesterol: 175 milligrams
Saturated fats: 8 grams
Polyunsaturates: 15 grams

POITRINE DE VEAU
(Sliced Breast of Veal)

2 ½ pounds breast of veal
salt and black pepper
2 tablespoons corn oil
1 medium onion, sliced
2 stalks celery, sliced
1 carrot, peeled and sliced
½ cup dry white wine
2 beef bouillon cubes dissolved in 1 cup boiling
*   water*

Pre-heat oven to 350°. Heat the corn oil in a Dutch oven or fireproof casserole and brown the veal on both sides. Cut into slices along the width of the breast. Season lightly with salt and pepper, add the vegetables and wine and cook over moderate heat until the wine has been reduced to 1–2 tablespoons. Add the bouillon, cover, and move to the center rack of the oven for 1 hour, or until the veal is tender. Remove the veal and vegetables to a serving platter. Trim the meat. Skim any fat off the liquid and spoon over the veal. Season to taste. Serves 4.

Calories per serving: 545
Cholesterol: 219 milligrams
Saturated fats: 7 grams
Polyunsaturates: 11 grams

RAGOÛT DE VEAU AUX LÉGUMES
(Ragout of Veal with Vegetables)

2 ½ pounds breast of veal
salt and black pepper
2 tablespoons corn oil
3 beef bouillon cubes dissolved in 2 cups boiling
   water
8 small white onions
4 medium carrots, sliced
2 turnips, sliced
2 stalks celery, sliced
4 ripe red tomatoes, quartered
1 tablespoon cornstarch
3 tablespoons cold skim milk } *mixed together*

Slice the veal into 1½ to 2 inch slices along the width of the meat. Heat the corn oil in a large, heavy saucepan, add the veal slices, and brown lightly over moderate heat on all sides. Add the bouillon, bring to a simmer, cover, and simmer 45 minutes. Add the vegetables, cover, and cook 30 minutes longer, or until all ingredients are tender. Stir in the cornstarch/milk mixture and cook over moderate heat until the liquid begins to thicken, about 3 minutes. Season to taste. Serves 4.

Calories per serving: 620
Cholesterol: 219 milligrams
Saturated fats: 7 grams
Polyunsaturates: 11 grams

LONGE DE VEAU RÔTIE
(Roast Loin of Veal)

> *1 boned veal loin*
> *salt and black pepper*
> *3 tablespoons flour* ⎫
> *3 tablespoons cold water* ⎬ *mixed together*
> *3 beef bouillon cubes dissolved in 2 cups boiling*
> *water*
> *½ cup canned button mushrooms*

Pre-heat oven to 375°. Season the loin lightly with salt and pepper and place, fat side up, on a rack in a roasting pan. Cook until done, allowing 20 minutes per pound, or until a meat thermometer reads 175°. Remove from oven, place on a platter, and cover with aluminum foil. Blend the flour/water mixture with the bouillon and bring to a boil. Scrape the pan drippings and add to the bouillon. Add the mushrooms. Simmer 3 minutes. Slice and trim the veal, spoon gravy over the slices, season to taste, and serve. Allow ½ pound per person.

Calories per serving: 410
Cholesterol: 175 milligrams
Saturated fats: 10 grams
Polyunsaturates: 10 grams

LONGE DE VEAU EN CASSEROLE

(Loin of Veal in a Casserole)

3 to 4 pounds loin of veal
salt and black pepper
2 tablespoons corn oil
½ cup water
16 small white onions
8 carrots, quartered
1 cup canned button mushrooms
4 ripe red tomatoes, quartered

Season the veal lightly with salt and pepper. Heat the corn oil in a fireproof casserole or Dutch oven and brown the veal. Add the water, bring to a simmer, cover, and continue simmering for 2 hours. Add the vegetables, cover, and cook 25 minutes longer, or until the veal is tender. Season to taste. Serves 6–8.

Calories per serving: 450
Cholesterol: 175 milligrams
Saturated fats: 6 grams
Polyunsaturates: 7 grams

FRICADELLES DE VEAU À LA NIÇOISE

(Veal Patties)

> 1 pound lean veal ground with 1 tablespoon corn
>   oil and ½ cup cooked rice
> 2 tablespoons corn oil
> 1 medium onion, minced
> 2 tablespoons tomato juice
> 1 clove crushed garlic
> ¼ teaspoon salt
> dash black pepper
> 1 egg
> all purpose flour
> corn oil

Heat 2 tablespoons corn oil in a skillet. Add the onion and cook until soft, about 8 to 10 minutes. Add the tomato juice, garlic, salt, and pepper, and cook 5 minutes over moderate heat. Pour the mixture into a mixing bowl, add the ground veal and egg and blend together thoroughly with your fingers. Divide the mixture in half, then half again, and half once more, and roll into 8 balls. Flatten these with the palm of your hand into 8 patties. Dredge in flour. Heat 3 tablespoons corn oil in a large skillet and brown the patties about 2 or 3 minutes on each side. Continue sautéeing until the patties are done, about 10 minutes. Turn only once and add corn oil if necessary. Season to taste. Serves 4.

Calories per serving: 430
Cholesterol: 150 milligrams
Saturated fats: 5 grams
Polyunsaturates: 15 grams

FRICADELLES DE VEAU DUXELLES
(Veal Patties with Mushrooms)

Follow the Veal Patties recipe (page 81), but add ½ cup finely chopped canned mushrooms with the egg.

Calories per serving: 440
Cholesterol: 150 milligrams
Saturated fats: 5 grams
Polyunsaturates: 15 grams

FRICADELLES DE VEAU AU THON
(Veal Patties with Tuna Fish)

Follow the Veal Patties recipe (page 81), but add ½ cup drained and mashed canned white tuna with the egg.

Calories per serving: 460
Cholesterol: 150 milligrams
Saturated fats: 6 grams
Polyunsaturates: 17 grams

PAIN DE VEAU
(Veal Loaf)

Follow the Veal Patty or Veal Patty with Mushrooms recipe (pages 81, 82). Put the meat in a lightly oiled loaf pan and bake until done, about 1½ hours. The meat will be a deep brown, and will have pulled away from the sides of the pan. Remove from the mold, slice, and serve with Tomato Sauce (page 28). Serves 4.

Calories per serving: 495
Cholesterol: 150 milligrams
Saturated fats: 5 grams
Polyunsaturates: 17 grams

FRICANDEAU AUX CHAMPIGNONS
(Rump of Veal in Mushrooms)

1 veal rump, 2 to 2 ½ pounds
salt and black pepper
2 tablespoons corn oil
1 sliced onion
1 carrot, sliced
2 celery stalks, sliced
2 beef bouillon cubes dissolved in 1 cup boiling
    water
1 cup canned button mushrooms

Pre-heat oven to 350°. Season the veal lightly with salt and pepper. Heat the corn oil in a saucepan and add the onion, carrot, and celery. Cook 5 minutes over low heat, stirring frequently. Transfer the vegetables to a roasting pan, arranging them along the bottom. Put the veal over them, add the bouillon, cover, and cook in the oven 1 hour, basting the veal with the liquid from the pan every 10 minutes. Move the veal to a serving platter. Slice, trim, and cover with aluminum foil. Pour the vegetables and liquid into a saucepan and add the mushrooms. Heat to a simmer, cook 3 minutes, then spoon over the veal slices. Allow ½ pound per person.

Calories per serving: 445
Cholesterol: 175 milligrams
Saturated fats: 6 grams
Polyunsaturates: 9 grams

SAUTÉ DE VEAU MARENGO

(Veal with Tomatoes and Mushrooms)

2 ½ pounds shoulder or breast of veal cut into 2
    inch pieces
¼ cup all purpose flour
salt and pepper
2 tablespoons olive oil ⎫
2 tablespoons corn oil ⎬ mixed together
1 clove crushed garlic
1 small yellow onion, minced
4 medium tomatoes, quartered
1 cup Marsala wine
¼ teaspoon each, thyme, basil, parsley flakes
1 tablespoon corn oil
1 cup canned sliced mushrooms
1 tablespoon cold water ⎫
1 tablespoon cornstarch ⎬ stirred together

Pat the veal dry, season with salt and pepper, shake in a plastic bag with the flour. Heat the olive/corn oil mixture in a large skillet and lightly brown the veal over moderate heat. Add garlic, onion, tomatoes, Marsala, and herbs. Stir, cover, and simmer over low heat about an hour, or until the thickest pieces of veal are tender. In a small skillet sauté the mushrooms in 1 tablespoon corn oil. Add the mushrooms to the veal and simmer one more minute. Pour the contents of the skillet into a sieve held over a saucepan. Put the veal and vegetables into a casserole. Heat the sauce to a boil, blend in the starch and water mixture, and simmer until the sauce thickens, then pour over the veal. Serve with rice. Serves 6.

Calories per serving: 470
Cholesterol: 150 milligrams
Saturated fats: 6 grams
Polyunsaturates: 11 grams

Vegetables

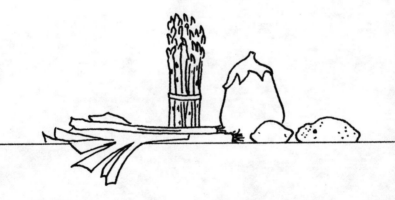

ARTICHAUTS PROVENÇALES
(Artichokes with Vegetables and Garlic)

> *4 artichokes*
> *¼ cup corn oil*
> *½ cup boiling water*
> *2 chicken bouillon cubes*
> *4 small white onions, diced*
> *4 small tomatoes, quartered*
> *4 cloves peeled, crushed garlic*
> *¼ teaspoon salt*
> *dash black pepper*
> *½ teaspoon chopped parsley*

Pre-heat oven to 400°. To prepare the artichokes, cut the stems close to the base of the artichokes. Lay them on their side and cut off the top quarter of each. Remove the small leaves at the base of each artichoke and trim off the remaining prickly points from the leaves with scissors. Wash the artichokes under cold running water.

Dissolve the bouillon cubes in the boiling water, stir in the oil, and pour into a casserole. Add the artichokes, onion, tomatoes, and garlic, sprinkle with salt and pepper, cover, and bake until the vegetables are tender, approximately 45 minutes. Sprinkle the parsley over the artichokes and serve with the vegetables. Makes 4 servings.

Calories per serving: 330
Cholesterol: trace
Saturated fats: 2 grams
Polyunsaturates: 8 grams

ASPERGES VINAIGRETTE
(Asparagus with Vinaigrette Sauce)

> 2 pounds fresh or one pound frozen asparagus,
>   cooked
> ½ cup Vinaigrette Sauce (page 29)

Drain the asparagus after it has been cooked, pour Vinaigrette Sauce over it, and serve. Serves 4.

Calories per serving: 120
Cholesterol: None
Saturated fats: 2 grams
Polyunsaturates: 7 grams

HARICOTS VERTS À LA CRÈME
(Green Beans with Béchamel Sauce)

> 1 pound frozen green beans
> boiling water to cover
> 1 teaspoon salt
> 1 tablespoon corn oil
> ¼ teaspoon butter flavor
> dash black pepper
> ½ teaspoon salt
> ¾ cup Béchamel Sauce (page 15)

Cook the beans in boiling water with 1 teaspoon salt until they are tender. Drain, add other ingredients, stir, heat, and serve. Serves 4–6.

Calories per serving: 85
Cholesterol: trace
Saturated fats: trace
Polyunsaturates: 3 grams

HARICOTS VERTS À LA PROVENÇALE
(Green Beans with Garlic, Tomato, and Herbs)

1 pound frozen, partially thawed green beans
1 cup diced onion
2 tablespoons olive oil
2 tablespoons corn oil
4 cloves crushed garlic
3 medium tomatoes, quartered
½ cup tomato juice
1 teaspoon salt
dash black pepper
¼ teaspoon dried parsley flakes
pinch thyme
pinch cloves

In a medium saucepan heat the olive and corn oil and add the onion. Cook over a small flame for 10 minutes, stirring occasionally. Add all other ingredients, except green beans and simmer for 30 minutes, stirring occasionally. Add the beans and simmer until they are tender, stirring occasionally. Serve hot. Serves 4–6.

Calories per serving: 110
Cholesterol: none
Saturated fats: 2 grams
Polyunsaturates: 7 grams

CHOUX ROUGE À LA FLAMANDE

(Red Cabbage with Apples)

1 head red cabbage
2 tablespoons wine vinegar
2 tablespoons corn oil
dash black pepper
½ teaspoon salt
pinch cinnamon
3 small tart apples, peeled, cored, and diced
¼ cup granulated sugar

Wash and clean the cabbage, removing all damaged leaves. Cut the cabbage into strips approximately ½ inch wide. Place in a casserole and sprinkle with the wine vinegar and corn oil. Toss lightly and sprinkle with the salt, pepper and cinnamon. Toss again lightly, cover, and cook in a pre-heated 350° oven for two hours. Combine the sugar and apples, sprinkle over the cabbage, toss once more, and return, covered, to the oven for one hour longer. Serves 4–6.

Calories per serving: 120
Cholesterol: none
Saturated fats: 1 gram
Polyunsaturates: 4 grams

CHOUX ROUGE AU VIN ROUGE

(Red Cabbage with Wine)

1 head red cabbage
3 beef bouillon cubes dissolved in 2 cups boiling
    water
1 cup diced onions
1 cup peeled, sliced carrots
3 tablespoons corn oil
2 cloves crushed garlic
2 cups red wine (Bardolino, Chianti, or Bordeaux)
½ teaspoon salt
dash pepper
pinch nutmeg

Pre-heat oven to 325°. Wash the cabbage and remove all damaged leaves. Cut into strips, about ½ inches wide, and set aside. Combine the onions, carrots, corn oil, and crushed garlic in a large saucepan or Dutch oven and cook over moderate heat for 10 minutes, stirring occasionally. Stir in the cabbage, mixing thoroughly with the other ingredients, and cook another 10 minutes. Stir in the remaining ingredients and transfer to a casserole. Bake covered for 2½ hours. Serves 4–6.

Calories per serving: 185
Cholesterol: none
Saturated fats: 1 gram
Polyunsaturates: 4 grams

CHOUX VERTS À LA BRETONNE
(Cabbage Breton Style)

> 1 medium sized head of cabbage
> 4 beef bouillon cubes dissolved in 1 quart boiling
>   water
> 2 tablespoons corn oil
> ½ cup diced white onion
> 1 sliced, peeled carrot
> 1 cup diced celery
> ½ teaspoon chopped parsley
> ½ teaspoon salt
> dash black pepper

Pre-heat oven to 350°. Wash and quarter the cabbage. Combine the oil, onion, carrot, celery, and parsley in a two-quart casserole. Stir in the salt and pepper. Place the cabbage quarters over these ingredients and add enough hot bouillon to cover half the cabbage. Cover and bake until the cabbage is tender, about 2 hours. Season to taste. Serves 4.

Calories per serving: 80
Cholesterol: trace
Saturated fats: 1 gram
Polyunsaturates: 4 grams

CAROTTES BRAISÉES AUX FINES HERBES
(Braised carrots with herbs)

> 1 pound carrots, peeled and sliced
> 2 tablespoons corn oil
> ½ teaspoon butter flavor
> ¼ teaspoon each, chervil, chives, and parsley
> ¼ teaspoon salt

In a saucepan, sauté the carrots in hot corn oil for three minutes, then cover and cook until the carrots are tender. Stir in the butter flavor, salt to taste, sprinkle with herbs, and serve. Serves 4.

Calories per serving: 90
Cholesterol: none
Saturated fats: 1 gram
Polyunsaturates: 4 grams

CAROTTES GLACÉES
(Glazed carrots)

1 pound carrots, peeled and quartered
2 cups boiling water
3 beef bouillon cubes
2 tablespoons sugar
1 tablespoon corn oil
½ teaspoon butter flavor
2 teaspoons chopped parsley
¼ teaspoon salt

In a saucepan, dissolve the bouillon cubes in the boiling water. Add the sugar, corn oil, butter flavor, and salt. Stir, then add the carrots. Cover partially, and cook over moderate heat until the carrots are tender, about 30 minutes. Serve hot and spoon the syrup over the carrots, and garnish with parsley. Serves 4–6.

Calories per serving: 60
Cholesterol: none
Saturated fats: trace
Polyunsaturates: 2 grams

CAROTTES VICHY
(Carrots Cooked in Club Soda)

Follow the Carottes Glacées recipe (page 93) but substitute club soda for the water.

Calories per serving: 60
Cholesterol: none
Saturated fats: trace
Polyunsaturates: 2 grams

CHOU-FLEUR AU SAUCE BÂTARDE
(Cauliflower with Mock Hollandaise Sauce)

1 head fresh cauliflower or 2 packages frozen
boiling water
1 teaspoon salt
Sauce Bâtarde (page 18)

Remove the outside leaves of the cauliflower, and cut the stem at the base of the head. Wash under cold running water and place the head in rapidly boiling salted water to cover. Boil slowly, uncovered, about five minutes. Cover and cook ten minutes more, or until tender. Remove cauliflower, drain, quarter, and serve with Sauce Bâtarde. Cook frozen cauliflower in accordance with instructions on package. Serves 4.

Calories per serving: 35
Cholesterol: 17 milligrams
Saturated fats: trace
Polyunsaturates: 2 grams

CÉLERIS BRAISÉS

(Braised Celery)

> 6 stalks celery, cleaned and sliced into 2-inch
>   pieces
> boiling water to cover
> ½ teaspoon salt
> 1 medium onion, diced
> 1 medium carrot, cleaned and sliced
> 2 medium tomatoes, quartered
> 2 tablespoons corn oil
> 2 beef bouillon cubes dissolved in ½ cup boiling
>   water
> salt and black pepper to taste

Cook the celery for ten minutes in boiling water to which the ½ teaspoon salt has been added. Drain. In a saucepan heat the corn oil and add the onion and carrot. Cook until onions are lightly browned. Add the celery, tomatoes, bouillon; cover, and simmer until celery is tender, about ½ hour. Season with salt and pepper to taste. Serves 4–6.

Calories per serving: 75
Cholesterol: trace
Saturated fats: trace
Polyunsaturates: 3 grams

MARRONS AU VIN ROUGE

(Chestnuts in Red Wine)

1 ½ *pounds chestnuts*
2 *cups boiling water*
4 *beef bouillon cubes*
1 ½ *tablespoons cornstarch*
3 *tablespoons red wine, such as Burgundy,*
     Madeira, Port, Bordeaux
1 *tablespoon corn oil*
½ *teaspoon butter flavor*
½ *teaspoon sugar*
¼ *teaspoon salt*

Slit each chestnut twice with a sharp knife; slit along one side of the chestnut about a third of the way through, then make another slit perpendicular to the first. Place the chestnuts in a roasting pan and set on the center rack of a pre-heated 450° oven for 20 minutes. Remove shells and skin as soon as chestnuts are cool enough to handle. As an alternative means of shelling and skinning, slit the chestnuts as before, then place in a saucepan of boiling water for 20 minutes. Drain and remove skins and shells as soon as cool enough to handle.

Set oven heat at 350°. Place peeled chestnuts in a casserole which has been oiled with the corn oil. Stir the cornstarch into the wine until it has a paste-like consistency. Dissolve the bouillon cubes in the hot water, then mix in the starch/wine paste. Stir in the salt, sugar, and butter flavor. Pour the liquid gently into the casserole with the chestnuts. There must be enough liquid to cover the chestnuts. Add more boiling water if necessary. Cover and bake until the chestnuts are tender, about 45 minutes. Serves 4–6.

Calories per serving: 205
Cholesterol: trace
Saturated fats: trace
Polyunsaturates: 1 gram

AUBERGINES À LA PROVENÇALE

(Eggplant with Tomatoes and Garlic)

> *1 large eggplant*
> *1 tablespoon salt*
> *½ cup all purpose flour*
> *1 clove crushed garlic*
> *⅓ cup corn oil*
> *1 teaspoon parsley flakes*
> *3 medium tomatoes, quartered*
> *salt and black pepper*

Peel the eggplant and cut it into ½-inch slices. Sprinkle both sides with salt and let stand for half an hour to remove water. Pat dry with a paper towel and dust with flour. Heat the oil in a large skillet, and add the garlic. When the garlic is brown add the eggplant. Fry over a moderate flame until each side is well browned. Remove with a slotted spoon and drain on paper toweling. Sauté the tomatoes quickly in the skillet, combine with the eggplant in a serving dish, sprinkle with parsley, season to taste, and serve. Serves 4–6.

Calories per serving: 165
Cholesterol: none
Saturated fats: 2 grams
Polyunsaturates: 8 grams

RATATOUILLE

*(Eggplant, Zucchini, Pepper, Onion,
and Tomato Casserole)*

>   1 large eggplant
>   1 medium zucchini
>   1 teaspoon salt
>   ¼ cup hot corn oil
>   2 tablespoons hot olive oil
>   1 medium yellow onion, diced
>   2 medium green peppers, sliced
>   2 cloves crushed garlic
>   3 small tomatoes, quartered
>   ¼ teaspoon parsley flakes
>   salt and pepper

Peel the eggplant and cut into ½-inch cubes. Remove
the ends of the zucchini and cut into slices. Combine the
zucchini and eggplant in a mixing bowl, sprinkle with salt,
and toss lightly. Let stand half an hour, drain, and pat dry
with paper toweling. In a large skillet sauté the zucchini
and eggplant quickly in the hot oil over a moderate flame.
Cook about 3 minutes then remove with a slotted spoon to
paper toweling. In the same skillet stir together the onion,
pepper, garlic, and tomatoes, and cook about 10 minutes
until the pepper and onion are tender. Place half the
onion/pepper mixture in a large casserole, and place half
the eggplant and zucchini over this. The remaining half of
the onion mixture is placed over the eggplant, and this is
then covered with the remaining eggplant and zucchini.
Cover and bake in a pre-heated 325° oven for 20 minutes.

Season to taste, sprinkle with parsley, and serve. May be served cold. Serves 6–8.

Calories per serving: 135
Cholesterol: none
Saturated fats: 1 gram
Polyunsaturates: 6 grams

POIREAUX BRAISÉS

(Braised Leeks)

12 leeks, white part only
3 cups boiling water
4 beef bouillon cubes
¼ teaspoon salt
2 tablespoons corn oil
¼ teaspoon butter flavor
1 tablespoon flour
1 tablespoon dry vermouth
½ teaspoon parsley flakes
salt and black pepper to taste

Dissolve the bouillon cubes in the boiling water. Blend the flour, corn oil, butter flavor and salt together and stir into the boiling bouillon. Lay the leeks in a casserole, add the liquid, cover with aluminum foil, and bake in a pre-heated 300° oven for 1½ hours. Season to taste, sprinkle with parsley flakes, and serve. Serves 4–6.

Calories per serving: 70
Cholesterol: trace
Saturated fats: 2 grams
Polyunsaturates: 6 grams

LAITUES BRAISÉES
(Braised Lettuce)

Follow the braised celery recipe (page 95) but substitute 1 head of lettuce, quartered. Garnish with chopped parsley.

Calories per serving: 70
Cholesterol: trace
Saturated fats: trace
Polyunsaturates: 3 grams

RAGOÛT DE CHAMPIGNONS
(Mushrooms in Madeira Sauce)

1 pound mushrooms
4 tablespoons corn oil
1 small onion, diced
⅓ cup Madeira wine
2 tablespoons flour
2 chicken bouillon cubes dissolved in 1 cup boiling
water
¼ teaspoon parsley flakes
salt and pepper to taste

Wash and dry the mushrooms. Heat 2 tablespoons corn oil in a skillet and cook the mushrooms and onion for 5 minutes over moderate heat. Add the wine and cook 5 minutes more. Drain mushrooms and set aside, saving the liquid. Stir together the flour and remaining 2 tablespoons corn oil and heat in a skillet until it begins to foam. Add the bouillon and wine liquid and stir over moderate heat until it begins to thicken. Add the mushrooms, cook an additional minute, season to taste and sprinkle with parsley. Serves 4–6.

Calories per serving: 20
Cholesterol: trace
Saturated fats: 1 gram
Polyunsaturates: 5 grams

SOUFFLÉ AUX CHAMPIGNONS
(Mushroom Soufflé)

1 tablespoon corn oil
1 teaspoon diced onion
½ pound minced mushrooms, cooked fresh or
    canned
2 tablespoons corn oil
2 tablespoons all purpose flour
1 cup hot skim milk
½ teaspoon salt
dash black pepper
1 egg yolk
4 egg whites
¼ teaspoon cream of tartar

Pre-heat oven to 375°. In a saucepan, heat the 1 tablespoon corn oil, add the onions, and cook over moderate heat until they soften. Add the mushrooms, cook two minutes more, and set aside. In another saucepan, heat 2 tablespoons corn oil, stir in the flour, and cook until the mixture begins to froth. Add the hot milk and continue cooking, stirring constantly with a wire whip or fork until the mixture thickens. Add the seasoning and the mushrooms, remove from heat, and beat in the egg yolk. Beat the egg whites until foamy. Add the cream of tartar and beat until the whites are stiff. Fold them carefully into the mushrooms and spoon into a lightly oiled 1½-quart soufflé mold or baking dish. Bake for 30 to 35 minutes, or until the soufflé has risen and the top is a golden brown. Serves 4.

Calories per serving: 170
Cholesterol: 63 milligrams
Saturated fats: 2 grams
Polyunsaturates: 7 grams

CHAMPIGNONS AUX FINES HERBES
(Mushrooms with Herbs)

½ pound large mushrooms
2 tablespoons corn oil
2 drops butter flavor
¼ teaspoon salt
dash ground black pepper
1 clove crushed garlic
1 tablespoon mixed herbs such as parsley, chives,
*   chervil, and tarragon, or parsley only*

Wash, dry, and quarter the mushrooms. Heat the corn oil in a saucepan and add the mushrooms. Cover and simmer for five minutes. Stir in the salt, pepper, and garlic, re-cover, and cook five minutes more. Stir in the butter flavor, sprinkle with herbs, and serve. Serves 4.

Calories per serving: 75
Cholesterol: none
Saturated fats: 1 gram
Polyunsaturates: 4 grams

CHAMPIGNONS NIÇOISE
(Mushrooms with Black Olives)

½ pound large fresh mushrooms
4 medium tomatoes, quartered
¼ teaspoon salt
dash black pepper
2 tablespoons corn oil
½ teaspoon parsley flakes
4 black olives, pitted

Pre-heat oven to 350°. Wash, dry, and quarter the mushrooms and place them, with the tomatoes, in a lightly oiled casserole. Sprinkle with salt, pepper, and corn oil and bake uncovered for 25 minutes. Sprinkle with parsley, add the olives, and serve. Serves 4.

Calories per serving: 110
Cholesterol: none
Saturated fats: 1 gram
Polyunsaturates: 4 grams

SOUFFLÉ AUX OIGNONS
(Onion Soufflé)

Follow the mushroom soufflé recipe (page 101) substituting 1 cup cooked, finely chopped onion for the mushrooms, and season with a pinch of nutmeg. Serves 4.

Calories per serving: 165
Cholesterol: 63 milligrams
Saturated fats: 2 grams
Polyunsaturates: 7 grams

OIGNONS BRAISÉS

(Braised Onions)

> *18 peeled white onions, about 1-inch in diameter*
> *3 cups boiling water*
> *4 beef bouillon cubes*
> *¼ teaspoon salt*
> *2 tablespoons corn oil*
> *¼ teaspoon butter flavor*
> *1 tablespoon flour*
> *1 tablespoon dry vermouth*
> *½ teaspoon parsley flakes*
> *salt and black pepper to taste*

Dissolve the bouillon cubes in the boiling water. Blend the flour, corn oil, butter flavor, and salt together and stir into the boiling bouillon. Lay the onions in a casserole, add the liquid, cover with aluminum foil, and bake in a pre-heated 325° oven for 1½ hours. Season to taste and sprinkle with parsley flakes. Serves 4–6.

> *Calories per serving: 110*
> *Cholesterol: trace*
> *Saturated fats: 1 gram*
> *Polyunsaturates: 3 grams*

PETITS POIS À L'ANGLAISE

(English Style Green Peas)

> *2 cups shelled fresh or 1 package frozen green*
> *   peas, thawed*
> *2 teaspoons granulated sugar*
> *boiling water*

1 tablespoon corn oil
salt and black pepper to taste

Combine the peas, sugar, and corn oil in a 1½-quart saucepan. Stir gently, then add boiling water to cover. Boil gently, uncovered, until the peas are tender, about 5 minutes. Drain and put the peas back in the saucepan and heat for a moment to dry the peas. Season to taste, and serve. Serves 4.

Calories per serving: 95
Cholesterol: none
Saturated fats: trace
Polyunsaturates: 2 grams

PETITS POIS À LA FRANÇAISE

(French Style Green Peas)

2 cups shelled fresh (about 2 pounds in shells) or 1
    package frozen green peas
2 tablespoons corn oil
8 small white whole onions, peeled
6 shredded lettuce leaves
1 tablespoon granulated sugar
½ teaspoon salt
¼ teaspoon dried chervil
dash parsley flakes
dash black pepper
⅓ cup water

Combine the peas, corn oil, onions, lettuce, sugar, salt, pepper, chervil, and parsley in a saucepan. Stir together and let stand 15 minutes. Add the water, cover, and cook for 20 minutes. Uncover and continue cooking until the liquid in the pan has been reduced to about 2–3 table-spoons. Serve. Makes about 4 servings.

Calories per serving: 160
Cholesterol: none
Saturated fats: 1 gram
Polyunsaturates: 4 grams

POMMES DE TERRE À L'AIL
(Potatoes with Garlic)

> 6 medium potatoes, peeled and quartered
> 4 cloves crushed garlic
> 4 teaspoons corn oil
> boiling water
> salt and pepper
> parsley flakes

In a saucepan, combine the potatoes, garlic, corn oil, and boiling water. Cover, and cook over moderate heat until potatoes are tender. Drain, add salt and pepper to taste, sprinkle with parsley, and serve. Serves 4.

Calories per serving: 160
Cholesterol: none
Saturated fats: trace
Polyunsaturates: 3 grams

POMMES DE TERRE PERSILLÉES
(Parsley Potatoes)

> 8 medium potatoes, peeled and halved
> 1 cup boiling water

2 chicken bouillon cubes
1 teaspoon salt
dash black pepper
1 tablespoon corn oil
parsley flakes

Dissolve the bouillon cubes in the water. Combine the liquid, potatoes, corn oil, pepper, and salt in a casserole, cover, and bake at 400° until the potatoes are tender, about one hour. Drain, sprinkle with parsley, and serve. Serves 4–6.

Calories per serving: 155
Cholesterol: trace
Saturated fats: trace
Polyunsaturates: 1 gram

POMMES DE TERRE SAUTÉES
(Sautéed Potatoes)

6 medium potatoes
boiling water
4 tablespoons corn oil
salt and black pepper

Boil the potatoes in a saucepan until they are tender. Peel and cut into approximately ¼-inch slices. Heat the corn oil in a heavy skillet, add the potatoes and fry until golden. Season to taste and serve. Serves 4.

Calories per serving: 250
Cholesterol: none
Saturated fats: 2 grams
Polyunsaturates: 8 grams

POMMES DE TERRE SAUTÉES À LA LYONNAISE

(Lyonnaise Potatoes)

> *2 pounds potatoes, peeled and boiled*
> *4 tablespoons corn oil*
> *2 medium onions, diced*
> *½ teaspoon salt*
> *pinch black pepper*
> *parsley flakes*

Cut the potatoes into ¼-inch slices. Heat 2 tablespoons corn oil in a skillet, add the potatoes, salt, and pepper and fry until browned. In a second skillet, heat the remaining 2 tablespoons corn oil and sauté the onions until slightly browned. Add to the potatoes, mix lightly, sprinkle with parsley flakes, and serve. Serves 4.

> *Calories per serving: 275*
> *Cholesterol: none*
> *Saturated fats: 2 grams*
> *Polyunsaturates: 8 grams*

POMMES FRITES

(French Fried Potatoes)

> *6 medium potatoes*
> *corn oil*
> *salt*

Peel the potatoes and cut them into rectangular pieces about ½ inch on a side and 2 inches long. Dry the potatoes and deep-fry in corn oil heated to 380° until the potatoes

are golden brown. Drain on paper towels, salt to taste, and
serve. Serves 4.

Calories per serving: 250
Cholesterol: none
Saturated fats: 2 grams
Polyunsaturates: 8 grams

CRÊPES D'ÉPINARDS
(Spinach Pancakes)

> *Ingredients for the crêpes recipe on page 126 (omit*
>   *sweetening)*
> *1 cup cooked spinach, puréed*

Combine the spinach and the crêpe batter and cook in
accordance with crêpes instructions. Serves 6–8.

Calories per serving: 67
Cholesterol: 22 milligrams
Saturated fats: trace
Polyunsaturates: trace

SOUFFLÉ D' ÉPINARDS
(Spinach Soufflé)

> *1 ½ cups fresh, or 1 package frozen, cooked*
>   *spinach*
> *4 tablespoons corn oil*
> *3 tablespoons all purpose flour*
> *1 cup hot skim milk*
> *pinch grated nutmeg*
> *½ teaspoon salt*
> *dash pepper*
> *1 egg yolk*
> *4 egg whites*
> *¼ teaspoon cream of tartar*

Pre-heat oven to 375°. Heat 1 tablespoon corn oil in a skillet. Drain and chop the spinach and cook in the corn oil over a moderate flame, stirring constantly until most of the water has been cooked out of the spinach. Set aside. Stir together 3 tablespoons corn oil and 3 tablespoons flour and cook in a saucepan until the mixture begins to foam. Add the hot skim milk, salt, pepper, nutmeg, and boil for 1 minute, stirring constantly with a wire whip, slotted spoon, or fork. Remove from heat and beat in the egg yolk. Stir in the spinach. Beat the egg whites until foamy. Add the cream of tartar and beat until stiff. Fold into the spinach mixture and spoon into a lightly oiled 1½-quart soufflé mold or baking dish and bake for 25 minutes, or until the soufflé has risen and the top is golden brown. Serves 4.

Calories per serving: 210
Cholesterol: 63 milligrams
Saturated fats: 3 grams
Polyunsaturates: 9 grams

ÉPINARDS À LA CRÊME

(Creamed Spinach)

> *1 ½ cups fresh, or 1 package frozen, cooked*
> *spinach*
> *4 tablespoons corn oil*
> *3 tablespoons all purpose flour*
> *1 cup hot skim milk*
> *½ teaspoon salt*
> *dash pepper*

Heat 1 tablespoon corn oil in a skillet. Drain and chop the spinach and cook in the corn oil over a moderate flame, stirring constantly until most of the water has been cooked out of the spinach. Set aside. Stir together 3 tablespoons corn oil and 3 tablespoons flour and cook in a saucepan until the mixture begins to foam. Add the hot skim milk, salt, pepper, and boil for 1 minute, stirring constantly. Stir in the spinach, cook for 1 minute longer, and serve. Serves 4.

Calories per serving: 185
Cholesterol: trace
Saturated fats: 2 grams
Polyunsaturates: 8 grams

ÉPINARDS BRAISÉES

(Braised Spinach)

> *2 cups fresh, frozen, or canned cooked spinach*
> *1 teaspoon corn oil*
> *1 tablespoon all purpose flour*
> *2 beef bouillon cubes dissolved in 1 cup boiling*
> *water*
> *salt and black pepper*

Place the spinach over a small flame in an enamel or stainless steel saucepan and sprinkle on the flour. Stir gently. Add the bouillon and corn oil, cover, and cook 15 minutes. Drain, season to taste, and serve. Serves 4.

Calories per serving: 65
Cholesterol: trace
Saturated fats: trace
Polyunsaturates: 2 grams

TOMATES À LA PROVENÇALE
(Tomatoes with Garlic, Herbs, and Bread Crumbs)

    4 red, firm, medium tomatoes
    3 cloves crushed garlic
    pinch thyme
    pinch basil
    ¼ teaspoon parsley flakes
    ¼ teaspoon salt
    dash black pepper
    ½ cup bread crumbs
    2 tablespoons corn oil
    2 tablespoons olive oil

Cut the tomatoes in half, scoop out part of their centers. Combine all other ingredients and fill each tomato half with the mixture. Place the tomatoes, cut side up, in a lightly corn-oiled baking dish and bake in a pre-heated 375° oven until the crumbs are lightly browned, about 15–20 minutes. Serves 4.

Calories per serving: 200
Cholesterol: none
Saturated fats: 2 grams
Polyunsaturates: 8 grams

TOMATES GRILLÉES
(Baked Tomatoes)

    4 firm, red, medium tomatoes
    1 tablespoon olive oil, 1 tablespoon corn oil, mixed
    salt and pepper
    parsley flakes

Wash and dry the tomatoes and brush them with the oil mixture. Sprinkle with salt and pepper and place in a lightly oiled roasting pan or baking dish. Bake in a pre-heated 400° oven for 15 minutes. Baste with the juices from the dish, sprinkle with parsley, and serve. Serves 4.

Calories per serving: 90
Cholesterol: none
Saturated fats: 1 gram
Polyunsaturates: 3 grams

NAVETS GLACÉS

(Glazed Turnips)

1 ½ pounds medium turnips, peeled and sliced
*   thinly*
boiling salted water to cover
2 tablespoons corn oil
2 tablespoons granulated sugar
2 beef bouillon cubes dissolved in 1 cup boiling
*   water*
salt and pepper
parsley flakes

Place the turnips in a saucepan, cover with the boiling salted water, and boil uncovered for 5 minutes. Drain the turnips, dry them in a towel and set aside. In a large skillet, heat the corn oil, add the turnips, and sauté them for 5 minutes. Dissolve the sugar in the bouillon, add to the turnips, cover, and simmer until the turnips are tender, about 25 minutes. Season to taste and sprinkle with parsley. Serves 4–6.

Calories per serving: 60
Cholesterol: trace
Saturated fats: trace
Polyunsaturates: 1 gram

Bread

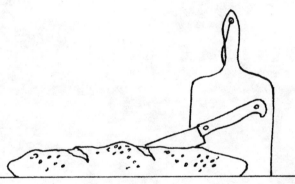

PAIN FRANÇAIS

(French Bread)

> 1 envelope yeast
> 1 ½ cups lukewarm water
> ½ cup skim milk
> 1 teaspoon corn oil
> 1 tablespoon sugar
> 1 ½ teaspoons salt
> 5 cups sifted bread flour

Stir the yeast into ¼ cup of lukewarm water. Scald the milk and add the corn oil, salt, and sugar. Let stand 10 minutes, then add the remaining lukewarm water and the yeast. Stir. Pour into a large mixing bowl and gradually add the flour. Knead until the dough pulls away from the sides of the bowl. Transfer the dough to a lightly floured board and continue kneading until the dough is smooth and elastic. Flour the board as needed. Place the dough in a lightly oiled bowl, cover it with a towel or cloth, and move it to a warm location (80 to 85° is ideal) until it doubles in bulk, about 1½ to 2 hours. The dough should be allowed to rise until a finger pressed deeply into it leaves a lasting impression. Punch the dough down, recover, and return to a warm location until it doubles again. This should take half as long as the first rising. Place the dough on a floured board and knead it about 1 minute, then divide it into two equal halves and shape each into cylindrical loaves. Place these on lightly oiled cookie sheets, cover, and move to a warm location until doubled

in bulk. While the loaves are rising, pre-heat oven to 400°.
Bake until the bread is golden brown, about 45 minutes to
1 hour.

Calories per serving: 100
Cholesterol: trace
Saturated fats: trace
Polyunsaturates: trace

PAIN ORDINAIRE
(Plain French Bread)

The traditional French bread. Use water instead of skim
milk, and omit the corn oil and sugar, in the French Bread
recipe (page 117).

Calories per serving: 95
Cholesterol: none
Saturated fats: none
Polyunsaturates: trace

DESSERTS

Some traditional French desserts like mousses, custards, and cream cakes are made with eggs, butter, and cream or whole milk, all of which are rich in cholesterol and calories. There are, however, many delicious French desserts such as soufflés, tarts, crêpes, savarins, etc., which can be prepared with corn oil, skim milk, and a minimum of eggs. Thus, the need to top off a good meal with something sweet can be satisfied without jeopardizing one's health. It is not necessary to give up or curtail what is to many people the best part of a meal. Furthermore, the weight-conscious individual can reduce calories even further by substituting artificial sweetener for sugar. In the recipes that follow some artificial sweetener is used to supplement sugar. Calories can be lowered even further by adding additional sugar substitute at the rate of one gram of sweetener for one tablespoon of sugar. Conversely, sugar substitute can be replaced in all recipes on the same basis—one tablespoon of sugar for each gram of sweetener.

MERINGUES AUX AMANDES

(Almond Meringues)

> 2 egg whites
> ¼ cup sugar
> 2 grams sugar substitute
> ½ teaspoon vanilla
> ½ teaspoon almond extract

Pre-heat oven to 250°. Cover a cookie sheet with brown paper. Beat the egg whites until they are very stiff. Gradually add the sugar and sugar substitute, continuing to beat the mixture as you do so. Add the vanilla and almond extract and beat another thirty seconds. Drop by spoonfuls onto the cookie sheet, or use a pastry bag and tube to shape the cookies. Bake about 45 minutes until the meringues begin to turn a delicate brown. Makes about 25 meringues.

Calories per meringue: 10
Fats and cholesterol: negligible

ROCHERS AUX AMANDES

(Almond Cookies)

> 1 cup all purpose flour
> 1 teaspoon baking powder
> 1 egg
> ¼ cup corn oil
> ¼ cup sugar
> 3 grams sugar substitute
> pinch salt
> ¼ teaspoon vanilla
> 1 ½ teaspoons almond extract
> 1 tablespoon crushed almonds

Pre-heat oven to 375°. Combine the oil, sugar, sugar substitute, and salt. Beat in the egg. Add the vanilla, almond extract, and almonds, and mix thoroughly. Sift the flour and baking powder together and add to the mixture, stirring until smooth. Drop by spoonfuls onto a lightly oiled cookie sheet. Bake about 15 minutes, until light brown. Makes about 20 cookies.

Calories per cookie: 62
Cholesterol: 13 milligrams
Saturated fats: trace
Polyunsaturates: 1 gram

GALETTES SABLÉES

(Sugar Cookies)

> 2 cups all purpose flour
> 1 tablespoon baking powder
> pinch nutmeg
> pinch salt
> 1 egg
> ½ cup corn oil
> 1 teaspoon vanilla
> 1 teaspoon almond extract
> ½ cup sugar
> 4 grams sugar substitute

Pre-heat oven to 375°. Sift flour, salt, baking powder, sugar substitute, and nutmeg together. Combine the egg, vanilla, almond extract, and sugar in a mixing bowl. Stir until smooth, then add flour mixture, and combine thoroughly. Roll into 1-inch balls and place these on an un-oiled cookie sheet. Flatten each ball gently with the fingers, shaping into cookies about ½ inch thick and 1½ inches in diameter. The cookies should be placed about 1½ inches apart. Bake about 15 minutes, or until the cookies are a delicate brown. Makes about 50.

Calories per cookie: 45
Cholesterol: 5 milligrams
Saturated fats: trace
Polyunsaturates: 1 gram

SAVARIN

¼ cup luke-warm water
1 envelope dry yeast
1 well-beaten egg
½ cup skim milk
¼ cup sugar
1 gram sugar substitute
pinch salt
¼ cup corn oil
½ teaspoon butter flavor
2 cups all purpose flour
½ cup white raisins

Stir the yeast into the water and let stand 10 minutes. In a large mixing bowl combine the egg, milk, sugar, sugar substitute, salt, corn oil, and butter flavor. Stir in the yeast mixture. Beat in the flour gradually. The batter will be soft. After all the flour is in, beat about 5 minutes, cover, and let rise in a warm location. If placed in an 85° environment the batter will double in about 40 minutes. After the dough has risen, work in the raisins with a wooden spoon. Empty the bowl of batter into a lightly oiled angel food ring, cover, and let stand 10 to 15 minutes, until the batter approximately doubles in volume. It will rise more quickly in a warm location. Bake in a pre-heated 375° oven for 20–25 minutes, until the top is golden brown, and a cake tester comes out clean. Allow to cool, then turn onto a plate. Spoon rum sauce (page 125) over the cake, and fill the center with strawberries before serving. Serves 10–12.

Calories per serving: 184
Cholesterol: 25 milligrams
Saturated fats: 1 gram
Polyunsaturates: 4 grams

BABAS AU RHUM

Follow the recipe for making a savarin (page 124) but spoon the batter into lightly oiled muffin tins, filling them halfway. Cover, allow about 10 minutes for them to rise to the point where they approximately fill the entire tin, and bake in a pre-heated 375° oven about 15 to 20 minutes, until the tops are golden brown. Allow to cool, and spoon rum sauce over and around the babas before serving. Makes about 20 babas.

RUM SAUCE FOR SAVARIN AND BABAS AU RHUM

> *1 cup water*
> *½ cup sugar*
> *½ cup white corn syrup*
> *¼ cup dark rum*
> *¼ teaspoon lemon extract*

Put the water, sugar, and corn syrup in a saucepan and simmer for 10 minutes. Remove from heat, stir in the lemon extract and rum, and spoon over savarin or babas.

> *Calories per serving, including sauce: 142*
> *Cholesterol: 13 milligrams*
> *Saturated fats: trace*
> *Polyunsaturates: 2 grams*

CRÊPES SUZETTE

1 cup all purpose flour
3 tablespoons sugar
1 gram sugar substitute
pinch salt
1 egg
1 cup skim milk
1 teaspoon vanilla

Put the egg, milk, and vanilla in a mixing bowl and beat thoroughly. Sift in the flour, sugar, sugar substitute, and salt. Stir the mixture, cover it, and let stand for 45 minutes. Crêpes are made in a frying pan which has been heated over a moderate flame and brushed with corn oil. Put about 2 tablespoons of batter in at a time, rotate the pan quickly to spread the batter to a diameter of about 5 or 6 inches, and cook about 1 minute. Turn with a spatula, and cook another minute. Crêpes should be as thin as possible. Keep warm on a hot plate, or in an oven set at 150°. When ready to serve, spoon warm Suzette Sauce over the crêpes. Makes 12–15 crêpes.

Suzette Sauce

juice and rind of one orange
juice and rind of one lemon
½ cup confectioner's sugar
1 gram sugar substitute
¼ cup water
2–4 tablespoons brandy (optional)

Mix all ingredients together and heat slowly over a small flame.

<table>
<tr><td>CRÊPES
Calories per crêpe: 60
Cholesterol: 22 milligrams
Saturated fats: trace
Polyunsaturates: trace</td><td>SAUCE
Calories per serving: 29
No fats or cholesterol</td></tr>
</table>

Beignets (Fritters)

BATTER

1 egg
1 tablespoon sugar
1 gram sugar substitute
pinch salt
¾ cup skim milk
1 tablespoon corn oil
1 cup all purpose flour
1 teaspoon baking powder

Beat the egg until it becomes frothy in a mixing bowl. Add the sugar, sugar substitute, salt, and corn oil. Stir. Sift the flour and baking powder together and add to the egg mixture. Stir lightly, until the flour has been thoroughly moistened.

BEIGNETS DE BANANES

(Banana Fritters)

Slice 4 peeled bananas lengthwise, then halve each slice. Dip pieces in batter, and remove, using a fork. Fry in hot

corn oil until golden brown. Turn once. The temperature
of the oil should be about 375°. Serves 4.

Calories per serving: 347
Cholesterol: 64 milligrams
Saturated fats: 2 grams
Polyunsaturates: 8 grams

BEIGNETS DE POMMES

(Apple Fritters)

Peel and slice 4 tart eating apples. Sprinkle them with ¼
cup sugar, toss lightly, and allow to stand for 30 minutes.
Dip in batter, and fry in hot corn oil until golden brown.
Serves 4.

Calories per serving: 332
Cholesterol: 64 milligrams
Saturated fats: 2 grams
Polyunsaturates: 8 grams

Tartes Sucrées (Dessert Tarts)

Tarts are small, open-faced pies. The filling is held by a
supporting shell. Sometimes tarts are partially covered
with a pastry lattice, but because these lattices add more in
calories than they do in aesthetics, they are best omitted.

Aluminum tart pans are sold in most supermarkets.
Although sizes may vary among manufacturers, the standard diameter for tart pans is five inches. Tart pastry is
crisper than pie pastry, and more durable. The recipe
below will make four or five tart shells, depending on the
thickness, which is a matter of preference.

TART PASTRY

> 1 cup all purpose flour
> 1 tablespoon sugar
> 1 gram sugar substitute
> ¼ cup corn oil
> ½ teaspoon butter flavor
> 2 tablespoons skim milk
> 1 egg white
> ⅓ cup all purpose flour

Sift together one cup of flour, sugar, and sugar substitute. Make a well in the center and add the oil and butter flavor. With the tines of a fork stir the oil into the flour. When all the flour has been dampened, add the milk and egg white, and mix. The mixture will be pasty. Sprinkle the remaining ⅓ cup of flour over the mixture, working it well with your fingers, until it is smooth and firm. Roll it into a ball. Divide the pastry into two parts, roll into balls, divide again, and roll into balls. Each of the four balls will be enough to fill a standard five-inch diameter aluminum tart pan.

Proceed to roll the pastry as follows: place each ball on a sheet of wax paper about 1 foot long. Pat the ball with the palm of your hand several times to flatten it. Cover with a second piece of wax paper, and roll it with a rolling pin. Work outward from the center. The direction in which you roll should be varied to keep the shape of the pastry approximately round. When the pastry has been rolled out to the proper size, about an inch-and-a-half larger than the pan, lift the top layer of wax paper gently away from the pastry. Lift the bottom layer of wax paper at one side and fold once so the pastry is doubled on itself. Gently peel away half the wax paper. Turn the pastry upside down, with the wax paper now facing up. Peel the other half of the wax paper away. Lift the pastry, which is folded double, into the pan, unfold it, and fit it carefully into place. Trim excess.

Because tarts do not have a top covering of pastry, the pastry should be tamped firmly along the sides and bottom of the pan, and pricked to allow any air trapped under the dough to escape. Bake on the center rack of a preheated 425° oven for 12–14 minutes. Do not place on a cookie sheet because the bottom of the shell will burn.

TARTES AUX CERISES GLACÉES
(Glazed Cherry Tarts)

>*4 unbaked tart shells*
>*4 cups canned, drained, tart cherries*
>*¾ cups sugar*
>*5 grams sugar substitute*
>*2 tablespoons flour*
>*4 tablespoons Currant Glaze (page 136)*

Place the cherries in a mixing bowl. Sprinkle the sugar, sugar substitute, and flour over them, and mix thoroughly. Spoon the cherries into the tart shells and bake in a pre-heated 375° oven for 50–55 minutes. Remove from oven and while still warm brush with currant glaze.

Calories per serving: 225
Cholesterol: 1 milligram
Saturated fats: 1 gram
Polyunsaturates: 4 grams

TARTES AUX PÊCHES GLACÉES
(Glazed Peach Tarts)

Follow the Glazed Cherry Tart recipe (page 130) substituting canned, drained, peach slices, and using ½ cup sugar instead of ¾, and 3 grams sugar substitute instead of 5. Brush the finished tart with apricot glaze (page 136).

Calories per serving: 225
Cholesterol: 1 milligram
Saturated fats: 1 gram
Polyunsaturates: 4 grams

TARTES AUX FRAISES GLACÉES
(Glazed Strawberry Tarts)

Follow the glazed cherry tart recipe (page 130) substituting thawed, frozen, drained strawberries for the cherries, using ½ cup sugar, 3 grams sugar substitute, and brushing with Currant Glaze (page 136).

Calories per serving: 256
Cholesterol: 1 milligram
Saturated fats: 1 gram
Polyunsaturates: 4 grams

TARTES AUX BANANES GLACÉES
(Glazed Banana Tarts)

Follow the Glazed Cherry Tart recipe (page 130) substituting four small sliced fresh bananas for the cherries. Use ½ cup sugar and 3 grams sugar substitute, and brush the finished tart with apricot glaze (page 136).

Calories per serving: 218
Cholesterol: 1 milligram
Saturated fats: 1 gram
Polyunsaturates: 4 grams

TARTE AUX POMMES

(Apple Tart)

4 unbaked 5-inch tart shells
3 large or 5 medium tart eating apples
⅔ cup sugar
3 grams sugar substitute
pinch cinnamon
¼ cup water
½ teaspoon lemon extract
1 tablespoon all purpose flour
⅓ cup raisins

Peel and slice the apples and put them in a mixing bowl. Dissolve the lemon extract in the water and pour over the apples. Sprinkle on the cinnamon, sugar, and sugar substitute, and mix thoroughly; dust with the flour, mix, then add the raisins, and mix these in completely. Spoon the apple mixture into the tart shells, and bake in a pre-heated 375° oven for 50–55 minutes. After removing from the oven, brush the tarts with apricot glaze (page 136). Makes 4 tarts, 8 servings.

Calories per serving: 241
Cholesterol: none
Saturated fats: 1 gram
Polyunsaturates: 4 grams

TARTES AUX FRUITS FRANÇAISES
(French Fruit Tarts)

Light, delicate, tasty desserts are made using a basic cream filling, topping this with fruit, and glazing. The basic cream filling recipe follows:

CRÉME À LA VANILLE
(Basic Cream Filling)

> 1 cup cold skim milk
> 1 tablespoon flour
> ¼ cup sugar
> 2 grams sugar substitute
> 1 egg white
> ½ teaspoon vanilla
> ¼ teaspoon butter flavor

Dissolve the flour in the milk. Place in a heavy saucepan over low flame and add the sugar and sugar substitute. Stir constantly until the mixture thickens. Beat the egg white slightly, and stir it into the thickening mixture. Continue cooking and stirring another 3 minutes, then remove from heat. Allow to cool about 30 minutes, then stir in the vanilla and butter flavor.

TARTES AU CRÈME PRINTEMPS
(Strawberry Cream Tarts)

> 4 pre-baked tart shells
> 3 cups thawed, drained, frozen strawberries
> Basic Cream Filling (page 133)
> ¼ cup currant glaze (page 136)

Fill the bottom of the tart shells with the cream filling, two to three tablespoons in each shell. Cover the filling with the strawberries and brush with currant glaze.

Calories per serving: 226
Cholesterol: 1 milligram
Saturated fats: 1 gram
Polyunsaturates: 4 grams

TARTES AU CRÈME CERISES
(Cherry Cream Tarts)

Follow the strawberry cream tart recipe (above) but substitute canned, drained, sweet cherries for the strawberries. Brush with currant glaze (page 136).

Calories per serving: 214
Cholesterol: 1 milligram
Saturated fats: 1 gram
Polyunsaturates: 4 grams

TARTES AU CRÈME DE PÊCHE

(Peach Cream Tarts)

Follow the strawberry cream tart recipe (page 134) but substitute canned, drained, sliced peaches for the strawberries, and brush with apricot glaze (page 136).

Calories per serving: 206
Cholesterol: 1 milligram
Saturated fats: 1 gram
Polyunsaturates: 4 grams

TARTE AU CRÈME D'ANANAS

(Pineapple Cream Tart)

Follow the strawberry cream tart recipe (page 134) but place a sliced pineapple ring over the cream filling and brush with apricot glaze (page 136).

Calories per serving: 217
Cholesterol: 1 milligram
Saturated fats: 1 gram
Polyunsaturates: 4 grams

TARTE AU CRÈME DE BANANES

(Banana Cream Tart)

Follow the strawberry cream tart recipe (page 134) but cover the cream with sliced bananas, and brush with apricot glaze (page 136).

Calories per serving: 202
Cholesterol: 1 milligram
Saturated fats: 1 gram
Polyunsaturates: 4 grams

GELÉE D'ABRICOTS

(Apricot Glaze)

> *1 cup sieved apricot jam*
> *1 tablespoon fruit liqueur (optional)*

Bring the jam to a boil in a saucepan, remove from heat, and stir in the liqueur. Apply while the glaze is warm.

Calories per tablespoon: 57
No fats or cholesterol

GELÉE DE GROSEILLES

(Currant Glaze)

Follow the apricot glaze recipe (above) substituting 1 cup currant jelly for the apricot jam.

Calories per tablespoon: 57
No fats or cholesterol

SOUFFLÉ À LA VANILLE

(Vanilla Soufflé)

> 1 ½ *tablespoons corn oil*
> 2 *tablespoons all purpose flour*
> 1 *cup skim milk*
> *pinch salt*
> ¼ *cup sugar*
> 1 *egg yolk*
> ½ *teaspoon vanilla*
> ¼ *teaspoon butter flavor*
> 4 *egg whites*
> ¼ *cup sugar*

In a saucepan, stir together the corn oil and flour. With moderate heat under the saucepan, gradually add the milk, stirring constantly. Add ¼ cup sugar and the salt, and stir until the mixture thickens. Remove from heat, and beat together the yolk, vanilla, and butter flavor, and stir into the milk mixture. Beat the egg whites until they are stiff, then beat in the ¼ cup sugar, adding it gradually. Fold the egg whites into the milk mixture, and pour into a soufflé dish or baking dish placed in a pan of hot water. Bake in a pre-heated 375° oven 35 to 40 minutes, until the soufflé has risen and the top is a delicate golden brown. Can be served warm or cool. Serves 4.

Calories per serving: 223
Cholesterol: 64 milligrams
Saturated fats: 1 gram
Polyunsaturates: 4 grams

SOUFFLÉS AUX FRUITS

(Fruit Soufflés)

Peaches, apricots, or strawberries can be used with the vanilla soufflé recipe to make a tasteful fruit dessert. Line the bottom of the soufflé or baking dish with drained fruit, then put the vanilla soufflé batter over it and bake in accordance with directions. If canned or frozen fruits are used, the syrup can be spooned over the soufflé when it is done.

Average calories per serving: 300
Cholesterol: 64 milligrams
Saturated fats: 1 gram
Polyunsaturates: 4 grams

SOUFFLÉ AU CITRON

(Lemon Soufflé)

Follow the vanilla soufflé recipe (page 137), but stir ¼ cup lemon juice and the rind of one lemon into the milk mixture.

Calories per serving: 238
Cholesterol: 64 milligrams
Saturated fats: 1 gram
Polyunsaturates: 4 grams

SOUFFLÉ À L'ORANGE

(Orange Soufflé)

Follow the vanilla soufflé recipe (page 137), but stir ¼ cup orange marmalade into the milk mixture before folding in the egg whites.

Calories per serving: 220
Cholesterol: 64 milligrams
Saturated fats: 1 gram
Polyunsaturates: 4 grams

SOUFFLÉ AU FROMAGE (I)

(Cheese Soufflé)

> *3 tablespoons corn oil*
> *3 tablespoons all purpose flour*
> *1 cup hot skim milk*
> *½ teaspoon salt*
> *pinch nutmeg*
> *1 egg yolk*
> *1 cup small curd cottage cheese*
> *4 egg whites*
> *¼ teaspoon cream of tartar*
> *1 teaspoon confectioner's sugar*

Pre-heat oven to 375°. Heat the corn oil in a saucepan. Stir in the flour and heat until the mixture begins to foam. Add the milk, salt, and nutmeg and continue heating for 1 minute, stirring with a slotted spoon, wire whip, or fork.

Remove from heat and beat in the egg yolk. Stir in the cottage cheese. Beat the egg whites until foamy; add the cream of tartar and continue beating until stiff. Beat in the confectioner's sugar. Fold the egg whites into the cheese mixture and gently turn into a lightly oiled 1½ quart soufflé mold or baking dish. Bake 30–35 minutes, until the soufflé rises and the top has turned a golden brown. Serves 4–6.

Calories per serving: 175
Cholesterol: 50 milligrams
Saturated fats: 2 grams
Polyunsaturates: 6 grams

SOUFFLÉ AU FROMAGE (II)
(Cheese Soufflé)

The cheese soufflé recipe (page 139) can also be used as a dessert, by following the recipe as indicated but sprinkling with granulated sugar immediately before serving.

Calories per serving: 205
Cholesterol: 50 milligrams
Saturated fats: 2 grams
Polyunsaturates: 6 grams

Index